OFFICIAL PRICE GUIDE TO:

Silver-Silverplate

AND THEIR MAKERS — 1865-1920

by
CARL F. LUCKEY

Author of
Official Guide to
Collector Prints

House of Collectibles
OFFICIAL PRICE GUIDES

Standard Book Number 0-87637-338-4
Library of Congress Card Number 77-94795
Printed in the United States of America
Copyright © 1978 by House of Collectibles, Inc.
Helton Drive at Rasch Road
Florence, Alabama 35630
All Rights Reserved

EAU CLAIRE DISTRICT LIBR

All rights are reserved. No part of this book may be used or reproduced in any manner whatsoever without permission, except in the case of brief quotations embodied in critical articles or reviews.

73513

EAU CLAIRE DISTRICT LIBRARY

FOR MY DEAREST PATRICIA

Who has endured countless stacks of books, papers, mail, etc., and a six-foot table in the living room for months and months. She has boundless patience and my love.

ACKNOWLEDGEMENTS

A book as complex as this one requires a tremendous amount of usually thankless effort on the part of many. Any attempt to name all here who expended extra effort is bound to be incomplete; if any are left out it is through oversight not intent.

Mr. Ed P. Hogan, Historical Research Librarian, the International Silver Company.

I cannot begin to give this man enough credit for all his gracious help to me. It seems as if I see his name in the acknowledgement in every other book in the course of my research for this book. It is obvious that all of us in the study of, appreciation, and preservation of American silver owe him a vote of thanks.

Special thanks to Mrs. Dorothy T. Rainwater for her generous help and permission to use many photographs and illustrations from her book "AMERICAN SILVERPLATE", co-authored by her husband, H. Ivan Rainwater, and jointly published by Thomas Nelson Inc. and Everybody's Press, Hanover, Pennsylvania. Others contributing help were:

Isobel Beattie, Photo Section, Victoria and Albert Museum, London; Susan Doran, Silver Department, Sotheby-Parke Bernet, New York; Crackerbarrel Press, The International Sivler Company, Meriden, Connecticut; Gorham Silver Company; Warden Cook, Huntsville, Alabama; Bill Schroeder, Collector Books, Paducah, Ky.

PICTURE CREDITS

Victoria and Albert Museum, London: page 68 through 80.

Gorham Mfg. Co.: 82, 89-91, 95, 111, 113-115, 129, 135, 137, 146, 148, 152, 154-155, 184, 187, 191, 200, 207, 209, 212-213, 226, 242-243.

Dorothy T. Rainwater: 87, 108, 110, 145, 205, 231, 236. (Many of the pictures contributed by Gorham and International Silver were also contributed by Dorothy T. Rainwater.)

International Silver Co.: 92-94, 97-99, 102-105, 110, 118, 123-125, 127, 130, 140, 149-151, 161-164, 180, 189, 194, 202-203, 208, 217-219, 224-226, 235, 237-238.

1888 Crooks Catalog: 82-84, 107, 109-110, 112, 117, 126, 128, 133, 136, 141, 144-145, 147, 153, 156, 161-162, 168, 174-176, 178-179, 182-183, 185-188, 193, 195-199, 204, 206, 214-215, 218, 224, 229, 232-233, 238, 244.

1904 Unger Bros. Catalog: 95, 152, 156, 165-167, 169, 172, 230, 234, 241.

NOTE

Every reasonable attempt was made to obtain permission to use materials and pictures in this book. In some cases attempts to ascertain the responsible individual or company proved unsuccessful. This was due to death, moving without leaving a forwarding address, or a company going out of business, etc. In these few cases the material was used in good faith.

TABLE OF CONTENTS

SECTION I

SECTION II

SECTION III

SECTION IV

SECTION V

SECTION VI

INTRODUCTION

The interest in collecting American silver and silverplate is rapidly expanding from an already widespread phenomenon to unbelievable proportions. Books on the subject are proliferating and dealers multiplying.

This phenomenal growth is due primarily to the increasing scarcity of old handwrought silver pieces and the enormous prices they command.

Because of the general lack of much real interest (in the past) of silverplated objects produced in the Victorian and Edwardian eras (1840-1910) and the relatively minor attraction to those who would melt objects made of precious metals down for the money, many of these pieces have survived. These are the pieces we find predominantly in the antique shops, junk shops, auctions, garage sales, and flea markets of today.

As the auction prices of good, genuine articles marked as made by the silversmiths of Colonial, Revolutionary War and pre-1899's America skyrocketed above the $10,000 dollar mark, the value of 1800-1801 American silver showed a concurrent rise. The prospect of the average collector, dealer, or private individual obtaining a piece made by a silversmith prior to the Civil War must be considered remote at best. Therefore this book concerns itself, in the main, with the silver and silverplate made in the period of 1865-1920.

A person collecting silver today has a wide and varied selection from which to choose. There is also a wide range of prices, so that even the connoisseur of modest means will find that there are a number of silver and silverplated items within his reach. Prices have risen a great deal in recent years, but they are still well below comparable 18th century antiques. The manufacture of silverplated articles, we have seen, was a development of this era. Many of the silverplated articles duplicate the traditional sterling shapes and are four or five times less expensive and further, are less expensive than today's silver, even though they are a hundred years old or more. Eventual scarcity, as a result of their growing popularity, may start to make their prices rise above present levels, but so far they are plentiful enough for this not to be much of a danger. Good Hunting!

AUTHOR'S NOTE

A word about price guides. All price guides are just that, guides. No one can publish a totally accurate and completely comprehensive current price listing for a number of reasons. The most obvious one is the inherent delay between the compiling of a list of prices, and the printing and eventual release of the list. Prices in the area of collectibles just simply do not remain static. Another important factor to consider is that of the tremendous number of variables affecting the price of each individual piece. These include, but definitely are not limited to: condition of the piece; whether it is part of an integral collection or set which shouldn't be broken up; the scarcity of the object at that particular point in time (there may have been a sudden increase or decrease in number available of the piece in question); the part of the country (prices vary greatly from region to region); the type of seller (private individual or professional dealer who after all must usually earn his livelihood from sales). The list is almost endless, but you can see that all these variables can have an enormous effect on each individual sale.

The prices quoted are approximate average Current Retail Prices or Price Ranges. In most cases extraordinarily high [or low] prices for exceptional pieces or sets are not considered. It is therefore possible to encounter a price which does not fall within the range published in this guide.

This book is not the last word. It would be foolish to try to represent it as anything more than a guide, to help the uninitiated buyer to recognize a bargain at the flea market, garage sale, or junk store, and to help the casual, or serious, collector to learn a little more about his collection and its value.

Carl F. Luckey

HOW TO USE THIS BOOK

The book is divided into several sections each of which is listed in the contents on page IV.

There is a large section in the front dealing with history, recognition, care of silver, and other useful general information. The remainder of the book is dedicated to current retail price range listings and illustrations. The categories of objects are listed alphabetically. Should you have difficulty locating an object use the index provided at the back of the book.

The book is a guide and an indicator to the current retail prices of silver and silverplate of the post-Civil War period 1865-1920. It will also help you to learn about the products and the makers of this period. The prices quoted are approximate average current retail prices or ranges for items in good to fine condition. (See paragraph 2 in Author's Note pg. 2) You must keep in mind that silver and silverplate has almost always served in a functional capacity in most households and so, despite care and polishing, inevitably will be found in a "used" condition. Museum quality pieces kept in locked cabinets are not the province of this book.

Learn all you can about design, construction, shape, hallmarks, maker's marks, makers, related metals, etc. Learn to appreciate the products of American silver arts and artifacts and, if you buy, buy what you like, what you want to live with and even use. With the help of this book you will buy knowledgeably and enjoy the double benefit of living with beautiful things around you and investing wisely.

HISTORY OF SILVER AND SILVERPLATE

The metal silver (Ag - scientific symbol for silver, derived from the Greek "argyros" meaning bright or shining) is referenced numerous times in the earliest historical books of the Bible. It was used extensively by the Egyptians, Assyrians, Phoenicians, Greeks, and Romans. It is usually concluded by historians and archeologists that silver was among the first metals used by early man, gold, copper and silver. Silver was probably discovered last of the three because it seldom occurs in a metallic, shining state, but rather as a sulfide which must be refined. It was likely discovered as the result of a forest fire in a silver ore rich area causing a natural refining process by heating the silver ore close to the surface and causing it to melt and flow in a pure molten silver form. This was probably the first method by which silver was purposely mined and likely occurred in eastern Asia Minor sometime prior to 3000 to 4000 B.C. Down through the millennia to the present silver has been mined and worked into a medium of exchange, utensils dedicated to both religious and household use, decoration, etc.

During the Middle Ages and the Renaissance silver was mined predominently in Hungary, Transylvania, and Spain. However, since the discovery of the New World, enormous quantities have been mined in Peru and Mexico. Large quantities can also be found in sea water. It is presently possible to refine sea water for its production. It is likely that oceanographic technology will one day make this process economically feasible.

Since the earliest times silver, with its natural beauty, has been primarily devoted to the service of splendor. A precious metal, silver lends itself excellently to the designs of the artist and craftsman. This has helped to make it one of the best known of the noble metals.

A Short History of "1847-Rogers Bros." and the International Silver Company

A book of any sort about American silver would be incomplete without reference to the development of the world renowned International Silver Company, for its history and that of its predecessors is, in itself, a history of America's silversmithing.

Early records go back to 1808 when a man named Ashbil Griswold, having learned his trade from the famous Danforth family, set up his pewter shop in Meriden, Connecticut.

Soon he expanded his business to include britannia ware and, around the middle of the 19th Century, he joined other independent makers of pewter and britannia ware to finance the Yankee Peddlers—resourceful men who traveled about selling and bartering. Meriden became known as the center for pewter, britannia ware and silver. Even today it is known as "The Silver City."

In 1852 Griswold's successors and associates, headed by Horace C. Wilcox, formed the Meriden Britannia Company, a move that united independent manufacturers and instituted better selling and business arrangements. Meriden Britannia Company was the leading spirit and a direct forerunner of The International Silver Company.

The story of International would not be complete without reference to the Rogers Brothers who developed the electroplating process in 1847. This brought handsome silver within the means of thousands of households in America. The Rogers Brothers became affiliated with the Meriden Britannia Company in 1862, thus uniting two famous groups of silversmiths. Since that date "1847 ROGERS BROS" has been one of the most International Silver Company tableware trade marks.

The company was incorporated in 1898. Through the years International has developed steadily to become the largest silverware manufacturer in the world.

WHAT IS SILVER AND SILVERPLATE?

Sterling Silver

Pure silver is too soft and malleable to be fashioned into strong durable and serviceable utensils, therefore a way was found to give it the required degree of hardness. This was the development of sterling silver. An alloy is made by adding copper, which can be added to silver without materially affecting its color. There are 925 parts of silver and 75 parts of copper in every 1000 parts of sterling silver. It was around 1850-1860 when the word "Sterling" was first stamped into silver to indicate that it was 925 parts silver. Prior to the accepted use of this standard, most reputable manufacturers (when they wished to identify it as such) would stamp their products with words such as "Coin Silver", "Coin" or "Pure Coin". This designation was used on products made around the second quarter of the 19th Century (1825-1850) to designate the quantity of silver was 900 parts per thousand or less.

Around 1868 most silver companies switched from the coin silver standard to the sterling silver standard and it is the same standard used to this day.

SHEFFIELD PLATE

Sheffield was produced for a period of less than 100 years; so that *real* Sheffield plate is actually quite rare and should not be spurned by collectors. The process of Sheffield plate was discovered in 1743 when Thomas Boulsover of Sheffield, England, accidentally fused silver and copper. When the two metals were flattened into sheets they could be handled like solid silver. This method lent itself well to the production of small objects such as buttons and buckles. It wasn't until Joseph Hancock, Boulsover's brother-in-law and apprentice, introduced a way of fusing silver to both sides of the copper sheet like a sandwich that it became possible to make silverware for the table, and large rococo objects were produced for the first time. Because of the greatly reduced cost of making Sheffield plate and the fact that it was not heavily taxed, as was solid silver, people of average means were able to grace their houses with silver wares.

The term *plate* can be extremely confusing in that English solid silver was called "plate" silver because it was from plates of solid silver that most pieces were fashioned.

With the advent of Sheffield plate came a natural confusion for it also came to be known as **plate**. Unsuccessful attempts were made to have marks on Sheffield plate clearly distinguishable from other silver. All this caused a controversy that raged for more than twenty-five years, until 1784. At that time a set of standards was established which permitted Sheffield plate to be marked. Before 1784 all marking of Sheffield plate was prohibited by Parliament.

No date markings are found on Sheffield. The craftsmen of Sheffield plate marked their articles with their initials from 1750 to 1784 when they were permitted by law to use an emblem with their names. By the early part of the nineteenth century the emblem alone can be found. Until it was forbidden in 1896, the mark of the crown was frequently used to indicate quality.

With the introduction of the electroplating process the Sheffield plate industry came to an abrupt end; almost 100 years after the discovery of the fusion process.

SILVERPLATE

Although the electroplating process was probably known before the English firm of G. R. and H. Elkington it is usually credited with the discovery about 1838 when they first took out various patents concerning the process.

In 1847 the process was introduced to the general public in the United States by Rogers Bros. of Hartford, Connecticut. The company began mass-producing plated silver articles by the galvano-electric method (electroplating). Unlike the Sheffield plate (amalgamated), this coated a thin layer of silver over a base metal.

The principal differences between Sheffield plate and silverplate are the method of applying the silver and the fact that the object of Sheffield plate is fashioned from the plated metal and the silverplate article is plated with silver *after* the object is fashioned from the base metal.

BRITANNIA AND OTHER BASE METALS

A discussion of silverplate cannot be complete without reference to the base metals upon which the silver is placed.

Britannia is a metal, more correctly an alloy, closely related to pewter but differing in its composition. It is an alloy of tin, copper and antimony as is pewter but contains no lead as does pewter. Britannia is harder and has a much more pronounced sheen. It is formed by stamping and spinning rather than cast as pewter, therefore lends itself more easily to comples shapes.

Other base metals used in silverplating are copper, brass and nickel silver.

Although Britannia was the most frequently used base metal in the early days of the silverplating industry, today nickel silver is *the* base most often used for quality products. Many of the pieces utilizing copper or brass as a base are lesser quality.

HOW TO IDENTIFY TYPES OF SILVERPLATE

To identify the various types of plating combinations, many pieces manufactured were stamped with letters that indicated the base metal and plating process used. Pieces were marked as follows:

EPNS	Electroplate on Nickel Silver
EPBM	Electroplate on Britannia Metal
EPWM	Electroplate on White Metal
EPC	Electroplate on Copper
EPNS-WMM	Electroplate on Nickel Silver with White Metal Mounts

This was in addition to the various makers' marks, dates, trade marks, catalog numbers, etc., found on American silverplate.

STANDARDS OF SILVERPLATE QUALITY

Reprinted below is a guide that appeared in the Jewelers' Circular Magazine in 1896. This is a guide to the silver quality of all plated ware being produced in the United States at that time. These numbers and figures are to be found stamped on the bottom of silverplated items made in the approximate period from 1870 to 1920.

From: Jewelers' Circular Magazine, 1896.

SILVER PLATED WARE

Note: Manufacturers of silver plated flatware, in addition to their trademark, stamp the quality upon their goods, almost all of them adopting the same signs and figures. These quality signs and figures are as follows:

A.I .... represents standard plate.
XII .... represents sectional plate.
4 .... represents double plate, tea spoons.
6 .... represents double plate, dessert spoons and forks.
8 .... represents double plate, table spoons.
6 .... represents triple plate, tea spoons.
9 .... represents triple plate, dessert spoons and forks.
12 .... represents triple plate, table spoons.

TESTING FOR SILVER AND OTHER METALS

There is no real practical way for the average collector to test for the amount of silver in an object. Only spectrographic analysis is accurate enough to differentiate between 925 parts per thousand (.925) and lower standards of silver. The test described *may* enable the collector to determine whether something is silver or another metal (easier done by look and feel in my opinion), but unless the tester is familiar with the various shades of brown produced by brass, lead, tin, etc., the results will be disappointing.

WARNING!!

Pure Nitric Acid is a dangerously caustic liquid. Do not let the acid come into contact with your skin or clothing and do not breathe the vapors. Severe and painful burns will result.

When mixing the testing solution be sure to POUR THE ACID INTO THE WATER. NEVER POUR THE WATER INTO THE ACID. A VIOLENT REACTION MAY RESULT.

TESTING FOR SILVER AND OTHER METALS

You can tell the difference between silver and silver-substitute metals. The way of determining the percentage of silver in an object made from some kind of silver alloy is shown in the chart below.

The standard testing solution is made of 1 ounce of potassium bichromate, 6 ounces of pure nitric acid, and 2 ounces of water. In an inconspicuous spot, place a drop of the solution. As it reacts with the metal, the liquid will change color. Wash off with cold water, and a stain that identifies the metal will remain. The table below shows the results when the solution is applied to various metals. Most drug stores or chemical supply houses can supply these ingredients.

TO TEST FOR SILVER*

A test solution made of:

Potassium bichromate....1 ounce
Pure nitric acid..........6 ounces
Water..................2 ounces

Will give this reaction on the surface of the metal tested:

A. (Metal)	B. (One minute color change of liquid)	C. (Color of mark on metal)
Pure silver	Bright blood-red	Grayish white
.925 silver	Dark red	Light brown (grayish)
.800	Chocolate	Dark brown (grayish)
.500	Green	Dark brown
German Silver	Dark blue	Light gray
Nickel	Turquoise blue	Hardly any
Copper	Very dark blue	Cleaned copper
Brass	Dark brown	Light brown
Lead	Nut brown	Leaden
Tin	Reddish brown	Dark
Zinc	Light chocolate	Steel gray
Aluminum	Yellow	No stain
Platinum	Van Dyke brown	No stain
Iron	Various	Black
9-carat gold	Unchanged	No stain

The color change of the liquid is shown in column B. The liquid, not the metal, undergoes a change of color during its action for the period of one minute.

Column C shows the type of stain left when the test liquid is washed off with cold water.

*See "WARNING" note on page 10.

SOME NOTES ON VARIOUS TREATMENTS AND STYLES OF SILVER AND SILVERPLATE

ART NOUVEAU— Sometimes described as the Modern Art movement in the manufacture of silver, Art Nouveau sprang into full flower from France. It is legitimately considered part of the Victorian era as it was considered significant and flourished between 1880 and 1905. However, English designs were well on their way to new and different designs well before the Art Nouveau style became so popular. It must be noted, however, that Art Nouveau was still reflected in many of their pieces. Silver by Tiffany was often made in Art Nouveau style. Indeed, Louis Comfort Tiffany was the United States' greatest exponent of the style. In the United States, the Art Nouveau period lasted from 1901 to sometime between 1910-1915.

MARTELE— The Gorham Company of Providence, Rhode Island, was always a leader in new design trends in the 19th Century and in 1895 introduced an Art Nouveau expression of their own called Martele. It was felt that the limit of mechanical perfection had been approached and that the art of silver manufacture was being sacrificed to mechanics. The company therefore developed a line of silverware in which a silver slightly softer and purer than sterling was used to emphasize the flowing qualities of more natural designs.

The company took certain of the best men in their shops and educated them to the new designs. The designs were unfettered by the conventions of historic styles but at the same time did not show the extreme qualities of some of the examples of Art Nouveau. The most important aspect of the new design was form and the decoration was taken almost wholly from natural or naturalistic forms such as waves of the ocean, flowers, fishes, mermaids, clouds, etc. All the pieces were individual and none could be absolutely duplicated, for each was totally hand made.

It was an extremely difficult and expensive proposition to develop the workmen to the point where they were able to turn out satisfactory pieces. The artisan was given a design and a flat sheet of the metal, and told to work it into the design entirely by hand.

It took three or four years before the first acceptable pieces began to be produced and then introduced.

Where at first most pieces were vases, bowls and tankards, Martele now encompasses entire dinner services and all manner of ornamental silver.

The very nature of its production makes such pieces essentially a work of art. It is the work of a man's hands unaided by machinery of any kind. The marks of the hammer are left apparent upon the surface imparting a soft, misty texture that cannot be attained any other way. It is costly silverware and will always remain so, for it is produced with the greatest skill and a great deal of patient labor. It cannot be doubted that for those who seek the individual and unique, who want a service which cannot be duplicated, the Martele must appeal.

Martele Punch Bowl and Ladle
circa 1895

SILVER DEPOSIT/SILVER OVERLAY

Victorian designs often incorporated glass as a part of the overall plan. The Art Nouveau movement contributed a technique of silver deposit on glass around 1893 whereby a design would become a silver silhouette or filigree. It is variously called Silver Deposit, Silver Overlay, or Silver Resist.

Pieces of silver deposit are frequently found monogrammed, but many articles can be found with none. The latter are preferred by dealers; however, the collector, perhaps not so concerned with resale, might enjoy the sentiment behind the initials if known or the beauty of the monogram design itself.

Briefly the technique is described as covering the entire glass surface with a thin layer of silver, then one of gold and a third of silver. A layer of resist varnish is then applied in the intended design, the uncovered areas are then etched out, resulting in the silver design.

There was a technique that was used to give the effect of a heavy silver overlay. Here, the glass was produced with a raised design and a thin layer of silver was painted on these raised areas. This technique is easily discerned from genuine silver overlay.

Silver deposit first appeared in the 1880's and had its heyday during a thirty year period from the 1890's to the end of World War I. While articles had previously been mounted with silver, it was not until electricity was invented that silver overlay—the fusion of silver to other materials—was possible. Many processes to accomplish silver overlay were patented and the collector would be well advised to acquaint himself with all of them.

Silver Overlay is still being produced; however, one can usually detect the old from the new rather simply. The old pieces tarnish, while the new ones are coated with rhodium to prevent the tarnish of oxidation.

The tarnish of oxidation creates beautiful contrasting effects when the surface areas of the old, heavy pieces are polished to a sheen and the recessed areas are left oxidized.

Martelé Silver Deposit Ewer

Silver Deposit Toilet
Bottle circa 1900

CARE AND STORAGE OF SILVER
AND SILVERPLATE

It is always best to store plated or sterling flatware in a box or drawer lined with a soft cloth treated to impart tarnish resistant qualities. If you do not use it regularly it should be wrapped in tissue and sealed in plastic bags to prevent excessive tarnishing from oxidation.

Hollow ware, generally not used quite as often or regularly as flatware, should be stored in the same manner. This of course is a decided disadvantage if one wishes to enjoy the beauty of old silver on display. The best way is to display the pieces in a glass fronted cabinet that is as airtight as can be reasonably be expected of fine furniture. Tucking a few pieces of gum camphor* in unobtrusive locations within the cabinet will help to retard the inevitable tarnish development.

The best method of day to day caring for silver is an immediate washing after use, in warm, soapy water (not detergent but soap), drying with a soft cloth and proper storage. It is the proper, repeated washing, tarnishing, and polishing cycle over the years that imparts the beautiful patina associated with fine old silver.

There are a number of good products on the market today for the care, cleaning and polishing of silver, but the collector must take care to use them properly.

There are liquid cleaners into which articles may be dipped, but most will not only remove the tarnish from intended areas but will also remove the tarnish in crevices and depressed areas which define the decorative details so well.

Be very wary of commercially available metal cleaners with an abrasive powder ingredient. Use only cleaners recommended for silver.

Don't overlook the necessity of polishing your silver after cleaning, for it is the polishing which restores the tarnish resistance properties.

*may be purchased at any drug store.

The following is a list of recommended products. They should be readily available. If you cannot find what you want, ask for a recommendation from a reputable and knowledgeable silver dealer or jeweler who stocks and sells fine silver.

Pacific Silvercloth
Hagerty's Silver Foam
Hagerty's Silversmiths' Wash
Hagerty's Fork Cleaner
Hagerty's Silversmiths' Polish
Tarnish Shield by the 3 M Company
Hagerty's Silversmiths' Gloves
International Silver Company Silver Polish
Gorham Paste Polish
J. Goddard and Sons Paste Polish

A NOTE ON RESTORATION OF SILVERPLATE

There are those who would have you believe that the replating of worm silverplate is to destroy its historical significance and its original beauty. To this I say NONSENSE. If it is old Sheffield Plate then yes, for Sheffield Plate was made by the fusion of metals but silverplate was originally developed through the electrolysis process of coating a base metal with silver (see page 60) and replating uses virtually the same. In the author's opinion, replating of old silverplate does not devalue it; on the contrary, it restores its beauty and enables its possessor to enjoy if for many more years.

HALLMARKS

There is a widely held misconception that the marks found on American silver are called "hallmarks". This is simply not so. In 1300 in England the hallmark was introduced by statute. It was a mark to be impressed on the work to signify official purity of the metal. The statute was to be enforced by Goldsmiths' Hall, London; thus the name "hallmark".

The United States has never had a silversmiths' guild hall. The nearest approximation was the Baltimore Assay Office which was in operation between 1814 and 1830. A series of assay marks and date letters was used but not true hallmarks. From the beginning of silversmithing in this country we have had silversmiths' marks and, from about the middle of the Nineteenth Century there have been trade marks, but never have there been any hallmarks.

Any collector of American silver must necessarily understand the system of marking. While there was no organized system, the usual marks found on early American silver are made up of the silversmith's name or initials, generally surrounded by a shape such as star, circle, shield, oval, etc. Often a personal device was added. With the increase of silversmiths there came a natural confusion from similar marks. Some silversmiths remedied this by adding the name of the city where he made it. Some later American silver is found marked by the jeweler or other company that sold it rather than or in addition to the silversmith or manufacturer.

By the early 1800's many fake hallmarks were being used in the colonies to dupe the buyer into believing he was purchasing a silver article made in England. Therefore you must be sure first that the mark on a piece of silver is indeed American.

While all this confusion and lack of a maker-date system can make validation of an article of American silver difficult and determination of exact dates virtually impossible, approximate dates can be ascertained by knowing the years the silversmith worked and the historical elements style and form of silver pieces.

AMERICAN SILVERSMITHS' MARKS

Reproduced below are examples of commonly used devices to surround the silversmith's name or initials.

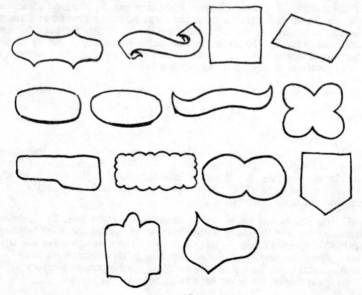

FAKE HALLMARKS / PSEUDO-HALLMARKS

Fake hallmarks and other pseudo marks were sometimes used to mislead or dupe the buyer. These were made to resemble the English silversmiths' guildhall marks. In the pseudo marks a star, hand, bird or a head was often used along with the maker's mark. In the case of the fake hallmarks they were outright copies of existing hallmarks or were merely fabricated.

A few examples of devices added to silversmiths' marks to make it appear to be a hallmark:

STANDARD AND ASSAY MARKS
AMERICAN SILVER

Generally speaking, the marks illustrated below were used from the end of the eighteenth century to the middle of the nineteenth. The reason for many of these stamps is not obvious. However, authorities* on the history of the marks used by the Baltimore Assay Office (see page 16) advise that from 1814 to around 1830, all assaying and stamping was very carefully supervised by specially elected silversmiths.

Maryland Silversmiths by Dr. J. Hall Pleasants and Howard Sill. *Old Plate* by J. H. Buck.

Standard and Assay Marks*

Standard and Assay Marks 1810-1850

*From: *American Silversmiths* by Stephen G. Ensko. Courtesy Cracker Barrel Press.

AMERICAN SILVERSMITHS AND THEIR MARKS—1800-1900

No listing and attempt at illustration of American Silversmiths and their marks has ever been complete. What follows here is a listing of many of the more commonly found marks. The first few pages are all illustrated marks arranged in alphabetical order according to the letters and/or words found in the actual mark. This is to enable you to find a mark more readily than in the often used method of listing the silversmiths in alphabetical order.

For example: if your piece bears the mark H & M you would look under the H's rather than try to determine what name the H stands for and search the lists for your mark.

Following the illustrations is a more expanded listing arranged in the same manner but the marks are described rather than illustrated.

Should you wish to obtain a more complete collection of illustrated marks for reference, please consult the "Recommended Books" section on page 54-56.

A

A. BEACH	**c 1823**
Hartford, Conn.	
ABEL BUEL	**c 1742-1825**
New Haven, Conn.	
A. C. BENEDICT	**c 1840**
New York, N.Y.	
ALEXANDER CAMMAN(Cameron)	**c 1813**
Albany, N.Y.	
A. CUTLER	**c 1820**
'Boston, Mass.	
ANDREW E. WARNER	c 1786-1870
A. E. WARNER, T. H. WARNER,	
A. E. WARNER, JR.	**c 1805**
Baltimore, Md.	
A. G. STORM	**c 1830**
Albany, N.Y.	

SELECTED AMERICAN SILVERSMITHS
MARKS 1800-1900

AHENDERSON	**A. A. HENDERSON** Philadelphia	c 1837
AHEWS,JR	**ABRAHAM HEWS, JR.** Boston	c 1823
A HOLMES	**ADRIAN B. HOLMES** New York, N.Y.	c 1801
A JOHNSTON STER	**A. JOHNSTON** Philadelphia	c 1830
A LOCKWOOD	**ALFRED LOCKWOOD** New York, N.Y.	c 1820
A.L.Lincoln	**A. L. LINCOLN** St. Louis, Boston	c 1850
AOSTHOFF	**ANDREW OSTHOFF** Boston, Baltimore, Pittsburgh	c 1815
APPLETON	**GEORGE B. APPLETON** Salem, Mass.	c 1850
A.RASCH&CO	**ANTHONY RASCH** Philadelphia	c 1820
ARNOLD JA TA	**THOMAS ARNOLD** Newport, R.I.	c 1790
A.SANBORN LOWELL	**A. SANBORN** Lowell, Mass.	c 1850
A.STOWELL.JR	**A. STOWELL, JR.** Baltimore	c 1855
A.T.BATTELS	**A. T. BATTELS** Utica, N.Y.	c 1847
AWHITE	**AMES WHITE** East Haddam, Conn.	c 1800

SELECTED AMERICAN SILVERSMITHS
MARKS 1800-1900

AWILLARD

A. WILLARD   c 1810
Utica, N.Y.

A&W·WOOD

A & W WOOD   c 1850
New York

B

Babcock

SAMUEL BABCOCK   c 1788-1857
Middletown, Conn.

BACHMAN

A. BACHMAN   c 1898
New York

BAILEY&KITCHEN

J. T. BAILY, ANDREW B. KITCHEN   c 1853
Philadelphia

BALDWIN&CO   **NEWARK**

ISAAC BALDWIN   c 1830

ISAAC BALDWIN, WICKLIFF BALDWIN   c 1830
Newark, N.J.

BALL·BLACK&CO

HENRY BALL, WILLIAM BLACK   c 1851
New York

BALL·TOMPKINS&Black

**HENRY BALL, ERASTUS TOMPKINS,
WM. BLACK**   c 1839
New York

BARD·LAMONT

CONRAD BARD, ROBT. LAMONT   c 1841
Philadelphia

BB BBENJAMIN

BARZILLAI BENJAMIN   c 1825
New Haven, Conn.

BENJAMIN BENJAMIN   c 1825
New York

BLEASOM & REED.

BLEASOM & REED   c 1830
Nassau, N.H. & Portsmouth, N.H.

SELECTED AMERICAN SILVERSMITHS
MARKS 1800-1900

BM BAILEY LUDLOW	**B. M. BAILEY** Ludlow, Vermont	c 1824-1913
B&N B&M	**ZEBUL BRADLEY &** **MARCUS MERRIMAN, JR.** New Haven, Conn.	c 1826
BOYCE&JONES	**GERADUS BOYCE & WILLIAM JONES** New York	c 1825
BOSWORTH	**SAMUEL BOSWORTH** Buffalo, N.Y.	c 1835
BRADY	**E. BRADY** New York, N.Y.	c 1825
BROWN&KIRBY	**BROWN & KIRBY** Philadelphia	c 1825
BRYAN	**PHILLIP BRYAN** Philadelphia	c 1803
B&R	**BROWER & RUSHER** New York	c 1834
BT&B	**BAIL, TOMKINS & BLACK** New York	c 1859
BW&Co	**BUTLER, WISE & COMPANY** Philadelphia	c 1845

C

CAPELLE ST.LOUIS	**JOHN PORTER CAPELLE** St. Louis, Missouri, Wilmington, Del.	c 1850
CB, CB	**CLEMENT BEECHER** Berlin, Conn.	c 1778-1869
C BARD 202 ARCH ST	**CONRAD BARD** Philadelphia	c 1850

SELECTED AMERICAN SILVERSMITHS
MARKS 1800-1900

Mark	Silversmith	Date
C.BILLON	**CHARLES BILLON** St. Louis, Mo.	c 1821
C BREWER	**CHARLES BREWER** Middletown, Conn.	c 1778-1860
CLB ❀ STERLING, CBoehme CLBoehme ❀ ❀	**CHARLES LOUIS BOEHME** Baltimore, Md.	1774-1868
❀ CC&D ❀	**CHARTERS, CANN & DUNN** New York	c 1850
C.C.&S.	**CURTIS, CANDEE & STILES** Woodbury, Conn.	c 1831
CDSULLIVAN	**CORNELIUS D. SULLIVAN** St. Louis, Mo.	c 1850
CH, CHEQUEMBOURG·JR	**CHARLES HEQUEMBOURG, JR.** New Haven, Conn.	1760-1851
CH CH	**CHRISTOPHER HUGHES** Baltimore, Md.	1744-1824
CH.PHELPS	**CHARLES H. PHELPS** Bainbridge, N.Y.	c 1825
CHURCH & ROGERS	**JOSEPH CHURCH, JOSEPH ROGERS** Hartford, Conn.	c 1825
C.&I.W.FORBES	**COLIN & JOHN W. FORBES** New York	c 1810
C.&J.WARNER	**C. & J. WARNER** Salem, Mass.	c 1825
CLARK NORWALK	**LEVI CLARK** Norwalk, Conn.	1801-1875
CLARK & BRO NORWALK	**CLARK & BROTHER** Norwalk, Conn.	c 1825

SELECTED AMERICAN SILVERSMITHS
MARKS 1800-1900

CLEVELAND WC	**WILLIAM CLEVELAND** Norwich, Conn.	1770-1837
COE & UPTON NY	**COE & UPTON** New York	c 1840
COOPER & FISHER 131 AMITY ST NY	**COOPER & FISHER** New York	c 1850
COWLES	**RALPH COWLES** Cleveland, Ohio	c 1850
Currier & Trott	**CURRIER & JOHN PROCTOR TROTT,** Boston	c 1836
CURRY & PRESTON	**JOHN CURRY, PRESTON** Philadelphia	c 1831
CURTISS-CANDEE & STILES	**DANIEL CURTISS, LEWIS BURTON CANDEE,** **BENJAMIN STILES** Woodbury, Conn.	c 1831
CURTISS & DUNNING	**DANIEL CURTIS & DUNNING** Woodbury, Conn.	c 1828
CURTISS & STILES CURTISS & STILES	**DANIEL CURTIS & BENJAMIN STILES** Woodbury, Conn.	c 1835
CWittberger CWittberger	**CHRISTIAN WITTBERGER** Philadelphia	1770-1851
CWESTPHAL	**CHARLES W. WESTPHAL** Philadelphia	c 1802
C.W.STEWART LEX.KT	**C. W. STEWART** Lexington, Ky.	c 1850
CWynn	**CHRISTOPHER WYNN** Baltimore, Md.	1795-1883

D

DARROW	**EDMUND DARROW** New York	c 1850
	or	
	JOHN F. DARROW Catskill, New York	c 1818
DAVID KINSEY DKINSEY	**DAVID KINSEY** Cincinnati, Ohio	c 1850
DAVIS PALMER & CO	**SAMUEL DAVIS, PALMER** Boston	c 1841
D.B.Thompson D.B.Thompson	**D. B. THOMPSON** Litchfield, Conn.	c 1850
D.B.MILLER DN	**D. B. MILLER** Boston	c 1850
* ꙮ *	**JOHN DeLAROUX** New Orleans	c 1882
D.GODDARD & SON	**D. GODDARD & SON** Worcester, Mass.	c 1845
DM , DMYGATT	**DAVID MYGATT** Danbury, Conn.	1777-1822
D.M.FITCH	**D. M. FITCH** New Haven, Conn.	c 1840
D.SULLIVAN&CO	**D. SULLIVAN & CO.** New York	c 1820
DTG ꙮ DTGoodHue	**D. T. GOODHUE** Boston	c 1840
DUHME	**DUHME & CO.** St. Louis, Mo.	c 1850

E

Mark	Name	Date
E. ADRIANCE	**E. ADRIANCE** St. Louis, Mo.	c 1820
EB E.B G.B EBURR E.BURR E.Burr	**EZEKIAL BURR** Providence, R.I.	c 1815
E.BENJAMIN E.BENJAMIN & CO.	**EVERERD BENJAMIN** New Haven, Conn.	1807-1874
E.BORHEK STANDARD	**E. BORHEK** Philadelphia, Penn.	c 1835
E.BRADY	**E. BRADY** New York	c 1825
E.C	**EBENEZER CHITTENDEN** New Haven, Conn.	1726-1812
E.COIT PURE.COIN	**E. COIT** Norwich, Conn.	c 1839
E.CUTLER	**E. CUTLER** New Haven, Conn.	c 1820
E.DAVIS E.Davis	**E. DAVIS** Newburyport, Mass.	c 1775
E&D.KINSEY E.&D.KINSEY	**E & D KINSEY** Cincinnati, Ohio	c 1845
E.H E.HART E.HART EH	**ELIPHAZ HART** New Britain & Norwich, Conn.	1789-1866
E.L LANG	**EDWARD LANG** Salem, Mass.	1742-1830
E.Lincoln	**ELIJAH LINCOLN** Hingham, Mass.	c 1820
EME	**EDGAR M. EOFF** New York	1785-1858

EMEAD	EDWARD EDMUND MEAD St. Louis, Mo.	c 1850
EOLLES&DAY	EOLLES & DAY Hartford, Conn.	c 1825
EP	EDWARD PEAR Boston	c 1830
E.Stillman	E. STILLMAN Stonington, Conn.	c 1825
E&S	EASTON & SANFORD Nantucket, Mass.	c 1816
E.Whiton	EZRA WHITON Boston	1813-1879

F

FELLOWS&STORM	FELLOWS & STORM Albany, M.Y.	c 1839
FESSENDEN	FESSENDEN Newport, R.I.	c 1845
F&H	FARRINGTON & HUNNEWELL Boston	c 1830
F.LOCKWOOD	FREDERICK LOCKWOOD New York	c 1845
FOSTER	JOSEPH FOSTER Boston	1760-1839
FORBES&SON FORBES & SON	COLIN V. J. FORBES & SON New York	c 1830
FROBISHER	BENJAMIN C. FROBISHER Boston	c 1834

SELECTED AMERICAN SILVERSMITHS
MARKS 1800-1900

Mark	Silversmith	Date
F S BLACKMAN / F.S.B&Co (·) DANBURY	**FREDERICK S. BLACKMAN** Danbury, Conn.	c 1832
F.S.Sanford	**FREDERICK S. SANFORD** Nantucket, Mass.	c 1830
F.W.Cooper	**FRANCIS W. COOPER** New York	c 1840

G

Mark	Silversmith	Date
GALE&WILLIS	**WILLIAM GALE, WILLIS** New York	c 1840
G.BAKER	**GEORGE BAKER** Philadelphia, Pa.	c 1842
G.B.BOTSFORD	**GIDEON B. BOTSFORD** Woodbury, Conn.	c 1845
G.C.CLARK	**GEORGE C. CLARK** Providence, R.I.	c 1824
GELSTON	**HUGH GELSTON** Baltimore, Md.	1894-1873
GELSTON LADD&CO NY	**GEORGE S. GELSTON & LADD** New York	c 1840
G.Eoff GEOFF	**GARRETT EOFF** New York	1785-1858
GEOW.WEBB	**GEORGE W. WEBB** Baltimore, Md.	1812-1890
G.GRAY	**G. GRAY** Portsmouth, N.H.	c 1839
G&H	**GALE & HAYDEN** New York	c 1840

SELECTED AMERICAN SILVERSMITHS
MARKS 1800-1900

GIBSON	**WILLIAM GIBSON** Philadelphia	c 1845
GILL	**CALEB GILL** Boston, Mass.	1774-1855
G.LOOMIS&CO ERIE	**G. LOOMIS** Erie, Penn.	c 1850
G.M.ZAHM	**G. M. ZAHM** Lancaster, Pa.	c 1840
G&M G&M	**GALE & MOSELEY** New York	c 1830
GOODING	**HENRY GOODING** Boston	c 1833
Gorham&Thurber	**GORHAM & THURBER** Providence, R.I.	c 1850
Gorham & Webster	**JABEZ GORHAM & HENRY L. WEBSTER** Providence, R.I.	c 1835
GOULD & WARD	**JAMES GOULD & WILLIAM H. WARD** Baltimore, Md.	c 1850
GREGG HAYDEN & CO	**WILLIAM GREGG, H. SIDNEY HAYDEN &** **NATHANIEL HAYDEN** Charleston, S.C.	c 1850
GRIFFEN & HOYT GRIFFEN & HOYT	**PETER GRIFFEN & WALTER B. HOYT** New York	c 1820
G.S.GELSTON	**GEORGE S. GELSTON** New York	c 1833
G.TERRY	**GEER TERRY** Enfield, Conn. & Worcester, Mass.	1775-1858
G.W.BULL	**G. W. BULL** Farmington, Conn.	c 1840

SELECTED AMERICAN SILVERSMITHS
MARKS 1800-1900

GW&H	**GALE, WOOD & HUGHES** New York	c 1835
GW&NCPLATT	**GEORGE W. & N. C. PLATT** New York	c 1820

H

H.A.McMASTER	**HUGH A. McMASTER** Philadelphia	c 1845
HARDY	**STEPHEN HARDY** Porstmouth, N.H.	1781-1843
HIGBIE & CROSBY	**HIGBIE & CROSBY** Boston	c 1820
H&M	**HALL & MERRIMAN** New Haven, Conn.	c 1825
H.L.WEBSTER	**HENRY L. WEBSTER** Providence, R.I.	c 1831
H.McKEEN	**HENRY McKEEN** Philadelphia	c 1823
HOBBS	**NATHANIEL HOBBS** Boston	1792-1868
H.L.W.&CO (Providence R)	**HENRY L. WEBSTER & CO.** Providence, R.I.	c 1842
HOSFORD	**HARLEY HOSFORD** New York	c 1820
HOOD & TOBEY	**BENJAMIN L. HOOD & TOBEY** Albany, N.Y.	c 1848
HP	**HENRY PITKIN** East Hartford, Conn.	c 1830

SELECTED AMERICAN SILVERSMITHS
MARKS 1800-1900

H.PORTER&CO	**HENRY C. PORTER & CO.** New York	c 1830
H.SADD	**HERVEY SADD** New Hartford, Conn.	1776-1840
H & S	**DAVID HOTCHKISS & ANDREW B. SCHREUDER** Syracuse, New York	c 1850
HUTTON ALBANY	**ISSAC and/or GEORGE HUTTON** Albany, N.Y.	c 1800

I

Jas Thomson	**JAMES THOMSON** New York	c 1834
I.BROCK NEW-YORK	**JOHN BROCK** New York	c 1833
I.FOSTER FOSTER	**JOSEPH FOSTER** Boston	1760-1859
IHL, JHL	**JOSIAH H. LOWNES** Philadelphia	c 1822
I I.L LYNCH	**JOHN LYNCH** Baltimore, Md.	1761-1848
I.McMullin SJMcMullin I.M·MULLIN I.M	**JAMES McMULLIN** Philadelphia	1814
J·MUNROE	**JAMES MUNROE** Barnstable, Mass.	1784-1879
I.N.TOY	**ISAAC NICHOLAS TOY** Abbingdon, Md.	c 1792

32

SELECTED AMERICAN SILVERSMITHS
MARKS 1800-1900

I.P.T.&SON	**JOHN P. TROTT & SON** New London, Conn.	c 1820
I.P I.P J.PERKINS	**JACOB PERKINS** Newburyport, Mass.	1766-1849
I.S.Porter	**I. S. PORTER** New York	c 1850

J

JABBOTT	**JOHN W. ABBOTT** Portsmouth, N.H.	c 1839
JACCARD&CO	**D. C. JACCARD & CO.** St. Louis, Mo.	c 1850
J.B.JONES J.B&JONES	**JOHN B. JONES & CO.** Boston	c 1813
J.B.M°FADDEN	**J. B. McFADDEN** Pittsburgh, Pa.	c 1840
J.C.M	**JOHN C. MOORE** New York	c 1840
J.CONNING MOBILE	**J. CONNING, WILLIAM A . CONNING** Mobile, Ala.	c 1850
J.CURRY J PHILA	**JOHN CURRY** Philadelphia	c 1831
J.DECKER	**JAMES DECKER** New York	c 1830
J.D.MASON	**J. D. MASON** Philadelphia	c 1830

33

SELECTED AMERICAN SILVERSMITHS
MARKS 1800-1900

J.FITCH ?

JAMES FITCH   c 1820
Auburn, N.Y.
JOHN FITCH   1743-1798
Trenton, N.J.

JEFFREY R.BRACKETT

JEFFREY R. BRACKETT   c 1840
Boston

J.J.LOW&CO

JOHN J. LOW & CO   c 1828
Boston

J.KEDZIE ☉ ⊕ ⊛

J. KEDZIE   c 1830
Philadelphia

J.L.MOORE J.L.Moore

JOHN L. MOORE   c 1835
New York

J.LORD J.LORD

JABEZ LORD   c1835
New York

J.L.W

JOHN L. WESTERVELL   c 1845
Newburgh, N.Y.

J.LYNCH

JOHN LYNCH   1762-1818
Baltimore, Md.

J.MEREDITH

JOSEPH P. MEREDITY   c 1824
Baltimore, Md.

JOHN B AKIN DANVILLE

JOHN B. AKIN   c 1850
Danville, Ky.

JOHN BIGELOW &Co

JOHN BIGELOW   c 1830
Boston

JOHN H. TYLER & CO

JOHN H. TYLER & CO.   c 1840
Boston

JONES BALL & POOR

JOHN B. JONES, S. S. BALL, POOR   c 1840
Boston

SELECTED AMERICAN SILVERSMITHS
MARKS 1800-1900

Mark	Name	Date
JONES LOWS & BALL	JOHN B. JONES, LOWS, & BALL Boston	c1839
Joseph T Rice J.T.RICE Albany	JOSEPH T. RICE Albany, N.Y.	c 1835
J.P.W	JOSEPH P. WARNER Baltimore, Md	1811-1862
J.SARGEANT	JACOB SARGEANT Hartford, Conn.	1761-1843
J.S.B J.S.B	JOHN STARR BLACKMAN Danbury, Conn.	1777-1851
J.S.SHARRARD	JAMES S. SHARRARD Shelbyville, Ky.	c 1840
J&W	JONES & WARD Boston	c 1809
J.WALTER	JACOB WALTER Baltimore, Md.	1782-1865
J.WARD HARTFORD , J.W	JAMES WARD Hartford, Conn.	1768-1856
J.WATSON	JAMES WATSON Philadelphia	c 1830
J.W.BEEBE J.W.BEEBE&CO	JAMES W. BEEBE & CO New York	c 1840
J.WEBB	JAMES WEBB Baltimore	1788-1844
J.W.F. J.W.FAULKNER J.W.F.	JOHN W. FAULKNER New York	c 1835

SELECTED AMERICAN SILVERSMITHS
MARKS 1800-1900

K

KG&J
KIDNEY, CANN & JOHNSON c 1850
New York

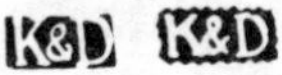

K&D   K&D
KIDNEY & DUNN c 1840
New York

L

LANG
WILLIAM LANG c 1844
New York

LANG EL
EDWARD LANG 1742-1830
Salem, Mass.

L.B
LUTHER BRADLEY 1772-1830
New Haven, Conn.

LEONARD
SAMUEL LEONARD 1786-1848
Baltimore, Md.

LH STERLING
LITTLETON HOLLAND 1770-1847
Baltimore

Libby Boston
JACOB G. L. LIBBY c 1830
Boston

LIDDEN
JOHN LIDDEN c 1850
St. Louis, Mo.

LINCOLN&FOSS
A. L. LINCOLN & FOS c 1850
Boston

LINCOLN&READ
LINCOLN & READ c 1835
Boston

LOW&CO
JOHN J. LOW and/or FRANCIS LOW c 1828
Boston

Mark	Name	Date
L. Walker, Jos Building	**L. WALKER** Boston	**c 1825**
L&W, STANDARD	**LEONARD & WILSON** Philadelphia	**c 1847**
LYNCH	**JOHN LYNCH** Baltimore, Md.	**1761-1848**

M

Mark	Name	Date
M.GORHAM M.GORHAM M.G	**MILES GORHAM** New Haven, Conn.	**1757-1847**
MITCHELL	**HARRY MITCHELL** Philadelphia	**c 1844**
MM MM MHM M M	**MARCUS MERRIMAN** New Haven, Conn.	**1760-1850**
MOORE MOORE	**JARED L. MOORE** New York	**c 1835**
MULFORDWENDELL	**JOHN H. MULFORD & WILLIAM WENDELL** Albany, N.Y.	**c 1842**

N

Mark	Name	Date
N.CORWELL	**N. CORWELL** Danbury, Conn.	**1776-1837**
NH H	**NICHOLAS HUTCHINS** Baltimore, Md.	**1777-1845**
NH&CO	**N. HARDING & CO.** Boston	**c 1830**

SELECTED AMERICAN SILVERSMITHS
MARKS 1800-1900

NATHANIEL MUNROE Baltimore	1777-1861
NATHANIEL SHIPMAN Norwich, Conn.	1764-1853
NATHANIEL VERNON (& CO.(Charleston, S.C.	1777-1843

O

O. PIERCE Boston	c 1824
OSMOND REED & CO. Philadelphia	c 1841
OBADIAH RICH Boston	c 1836

P

PHILIP BENJAMIN SADTLER Baltimore	c 1850
JOHN O. PITKIN East Hartford, Conn.	1803-1891
G. W. & N. C. PLATT New York	c 1820
PETER L. KRIDER Philadelphia	c 1850
PHILIP BENJAMINE SADTLER Baltimore	c 1850

SELECTED AMERICAN SILVERSMITHS
MARKS 1800-1900

R

RB	**ROSWELL BARTHOLOMEW** Hartford, Conn.	1781-1830
R&AC	**ROBERT & ANDREW CAMPBELL** Baltimore, Md.	c 1853
R.A.LYTLE	**R. A. LYTLE** Baltimore	c 1825
R·Gray ROBT GRAY	**ROBERT GRAY** Portsmouth, N.H.	c 1830
R.KEYWORTH	**ROBERT KEYWORTH** Washington, D.C.	c 1832
R·M R.MERRIMAN PureCoin	**REUBEN MERRIMAN** Litchfield, Conn.	1783-1860
R·RAIT	**ROBERT RAIT** New York	c 1830

S

SA SA	**SAMUEL AVERY** Preston, Conn.	1760-1836
SAM.KIRK SK H SK SK H S.KIRK SamKirk S.KIRK SKirk	**SAMUEL KIRK** Baltimore, Md.	1792-1872
SB BARRY	**STANDISH BARRY** Baltimore, Md.	1763-1844
S.BAKER C	**SAMUEL BAKER** New York	1787-1858

SELECTED AMERICAN SILVERSMITHS
MARKS 1800-1900

S·Bowne S·Bowne	**SAMUEL BOWNE** c 1778 New York
S.COLLINS UTICA	**SELDEN COLLINS, JR.,** 1819-1885 Utica, N.Y.
SCOVIL & KINSEY	**SCOVIL & KINSEY** c 1830 Cincinnati, Ohio
S&C	**CHARLES STORRS & OLIVER B. COOLEY** c 1832 Utica, N.Y.
S.D.BROWER	**S. D. BROWER** c 1834 Albany, N.Y.
S.D.ROCKWELL NEW YORK	**SAMUEL D. ROCKWELL** c 1825 New York
& SEYMOUR & HOLLISTER & S.F.YOUNG LACONIA.NH	**OLIVER D. SEYMOUR & HOLLISTER** c 1850 Hartford, Conn.
SH SH	**STEPHEN HARDY** 1781-1843 Portsmouth, N.H.
SHAW & DUNLEVEY PHILA	**SHAW & ROBERT DUNLEVEY** c 1833 Philadelphia
S.HOYT SHOYT PEARL ST S.HOYT & CO	**SEYMOUR HOYT** c 1842 New York
S.HUNTINGTON	**S. HUNTINGTON** c 1850 Portland, Maine
S.LEONARD	**SAMUEL T. LEONARD** 1786-1848 Baltimore, Md.
S.L.PRESTON	**STEPHEN L. PRESTON** c 1849 Newburgh, New York
S.MARBLE	**SIMEON MARBLE** 1776-1856 New Haven, Conn.

SELECTED AMERICAN SILVERSMITHS
MARKS 1800-1900

Mark	Name	Date
Smith & Grant	**RICHARD EWING SMITH & WILLIAM GRANT** Philadelphia	**c 1830**
S.P.SQUIRE	**S. P. SQUIRE** New York	**c 1835**
SQUIRE & BROTHER OF COIN	**SQUIRE & BROTHER** New York	**c 1846**
SQUIRE & LANDER	**SQUIRE & LANDER** New York	**c 1840**
SREED SREED	**STEPHEN REED** Philadelphia	**c 1840**
Standish Barry	**STANDISH BARRY** Baltimore, Md.	**1763-1844**
STANTON	**ZEBULON STANTON** Stonington, Conn.	**1753-1828**
STEPHENSON	**THOMAS STEPHENSON** Buffalo, N.Y.	**c 1840**
STOCKMAN & PEPPER	**STOCK(ER)MAN & PEPPER** Philadelphia	**c 1840**
SWILMOT	**SAMUEL WILMOT** New Haven, Conn.	**1777-1846**

T

Mark	Name	Date
TA TA ARNOLD **TARNOLD TA TA**	**THOMAS ARNOLD** Newport, R.I.	**1739-1828**
TAYLOR & LAWRIE	**ROBERT D. LAWRIE & TAYLOR** Philadelphia	**c 1841**
TENNEY 251 BWAY	**WILLIAM I. TENNEY** New York	**c 1840**

SELECTED AMERICAN SILVERSMITHS
MARKS 1800-1900

Th.Farnam	**THOMAS FARNAM** Boston	**c 1830**
T.K.MARSH PARIS.KY	**THOMAS KING MARSH** Paris, Ky.	**c 1830**
T.W STERLING ⦿ T.WARNER STERLING ⦿	**THOMAS H. WARNER** Baltimore, Md.	**1780-1828**

U, V

Villard VILLARD	**R. H. L. VILLARD** Georgetown, Md.	**c 1833**
V.LAFORME.	**VINCENT LAFORME** Boston	**c 1850**
V&W	**VanNESS & WATERMAN** New York	**c 1835**

W

W.ADAMS NEW-YORK	**WILLIAM ADAMS** New York	**c 1842**
W.A.RASCH NEWORLEANS	**W. A. RASCH** New Orleans, La.	**c 1832**
WARD HARTFORT	**JAMES WARD** Hartford, Conn.	**1768-1856**
WATSON&BROWN	**WATSON & BROWN** Philadelphia	**c 1825**
W.A.WILLIAMS	**WILLIAM A. WILLIAMS** Washington, D.C.	**c 1829**
WC.DUSENBERRY.	**WILLIAM C. DUSENBERRY** New York	**c 1830**

SELECTED AMERICAN SILVERSMITHS
MARKS 1800-1900

Mark	Name	Date
W.C WC	**WILLIAM CLEVELAND** New London, Conn.	1770-1837
WELLES&GELSTON	**WELLES & GELSTON** New York	c 1840
WENTWORTH&CO	**WENTWORTH & CO.** New York	c 1850
W.FORBES NY NY WF &CO NEW YORK	**WILLIAM FORBES** New York	c 1830
W&G.SHARP	**WILLIAM & GEORGE SHARP** Philadelphia	c 1850
W&H	**WOOD & HUGHES** New York	c 1846
WILMOT	**SAMUEL WILMOT** New Haven, Conn.	c 1800
⬤ WJ ⬤	**WILLIAM B. JOHONNOT** Middletown, Conn.	1766-1849
WKENDRICK LOUISVILLE	**WILLIAM KENDRICK** Louisville, Ky.	c 1840
Wm.B.Durgin CONCORD.N.H	**WILLIAM B. DURGIN** Concord, N.H.	c 1850
W.M°P	**WILLIAM McPARLIN** Annapolis, Md.	1780-1850
W°ROGERS HARTFORD	**WILLIAM ROGERS** Hartford, Conn.	1801-1873
WM.ROGERS&SON	**WILLIAM ROGERS & SON** Hartford, Conn.	c 1850
W°W·WHITE	**WILLIAM W. WHITE** New York	c 1835

SELECTED AMERICAN SILVERSMITHS
MARKS 1800-1900

W. N. ROOT & BROTHER   c 1850
New Haven, Conn.

WOLFE & WRIGGINS   c 1837
Philadelphia

JACOB WOOD & JASPER W. HUGHES c 1845
New York

WALTER PITKIN   1808-1885
East Hartford, Conn.

WILLIAM B. NORTH   1787-1838
New York

WILLIAM S. NICHOL   1785-1871
Newport, R.I.

WILLIAM SMITH PELLETREAU   1786-1842
Southampton, L.I., New York

W. W. GASKINS   c 1830
Providence, R.I.

WILLIAM WARD   1742-1828
Litchfield, Conn.

WYER & FARLEY   1828-1832
Portland, Maine

X, Y, Z

ZAHM & JACKSON   c 1830
New York

ZEBULON SMITH   1786-1865
Maine

SELECTED AMERICAN SILVERSMITHS MARKS
1800-1900 (Expanded List)

Mark	Silversmith	City & State	Date	Type of Marks
AB	Abel Buel	New Haven, Conn.	1742-1825	Elongated oval punch
AC	Alexander Camman	Albany, N.Y.	Early 1800's	Oblong punch
AC	Aaron Cleveland	Norwich, Conn.	About 1820	Oblong punch-tilted corners
AC	Albert Cole	New York, N.Y.		
AD	Amos Doolittle	New Haven, Conn.	1754-1832	Oval punch
A-E-W	Andrew E. Warner	Baltimore, Md.	1786-1870	Oblong punch-serrated ends; also in plain oblong punch AEW with interlaced italic caps
A & G.W.	A. & G. Welles	Boston, Mass.	Early 1800's	Oblong punch
A.J.&Co.	A. Jacobs & Co.	Philadelphia, Pa.	Circa, 1820	Oblong punch
BB	Benjamin Bussey	Dedham, Mass.	1757-1842	Oblong punch
BB	Benjamin Benjamin	New York, N.Y.	Circa, 1825	Oblong punch-tilted corners, or incised
B & D	Barrington & Davenport	Philadelphia, Pa.	Circa, 1805	Oblong punch-Serrated edged
B.G.	Baldwin Gardiner	Philadelphia, Pa.	Circa, 1814	Oblong punch
B.G & Co.	B. Gardiner & Co.	New York, N.Y.	Circa, 1836	Oblong punch
B&I or B&J	Boyce & Jones	New York, N.Y.	Circa, 1825	Both in oblong punch
B & M	Bradley & Merriman	New Haven, Conn.	Circa, 1825	Shaped to include star or oblong punch
B & R	Brower & Rusher	New York, N.Y.	About 1834	Oblong punch
B T & B	Ball, Tompkins & Black	New York, N.Y.	Circa, 1839	Oblong punch
BW & Co.	Butler, Wise & Co.	Philadelphia, Pa.	About 1845	Oblong-rounded end

SELECTED AMERICAN SILVERSMITHS MARKS
1800-1900

Mark	Silversmith	City & State	Date	Type of Marks
CB	Clement Beecher	Berlin, Conn.	1778-1869	Oblong or rounded punch-serrated edges
CC	Christian Cornelius	Philadelphia, Pa.	About 1810	Oblong punch
CC & D	Charters, Cann & Dunn	New York, N.Y.	About 1850	Oblong punch
CC & S	Curtis, Candee & Stiles	Woodbury, Conn.	About 1840	Oblong punch
CH	Charles Hequembourg, Jr.	New Haven, Conn.	1760-1851	Shaped punch
CH	Christopher Hughes	Baltimore, Md.	1744-1824	Oblong punch
CL	Charles Leach	Boston, Mass.	1765-1814	Oblong punch-waved edges
CLB	Charles L. Boehme	Baltimore, Md.	1774-1868	Oblong punch
C&M	Coit & Mansfield	Norwich, Conn.	About 1816	Oblong punch-also with rounded ends
C&P	Cleveland & Post	Norwich, Conn.	Circa, 1815	Oblong punch-also with serrated edges
C&P	Curry & Preston	Philadelphia, Pa.	About 1831	Oblong punch
CVGF or C.V.G.F.	Collins V. G. Forbes	New York, N.Y.	About 1816	Oblong punch
C.W.	Christian Wiltberger	Philadelphia, Pa.	1770-1851	Oblong punch
D:D or DD	Daniel Dupuy	Philadelphia, Pa.	1719-1807	Oblong, shaped or oval punch
DM	David Mygatt	Danbury, Conn.	1777-1822	Oblong punch
DM	David Moseley	Boston, Mass.	1753-1812	Oblong punch
DN	David I. Northee	Salem, Mass.	d. 1788	Oblong punch
D&P	Downing & Phelps	New York, N.Y.	About 1810	Oblong punch
D.T.G.	D.T. Goodhue	Boston, Mass.	fl. 1840's	Oblong punch
D&W	Davis & Watson	Boston, Mass.	Circa, 1815	Oblong punch with italic caps
EB	Ezekial Burr	Providence, R.I.	1764-1846	EB in italic caps, shaped or oval punch-also oblong punch

SELECTED AMERICAN SILVERSMITHS MARKS
1800-1900

Mark	Silversmith	City & State	Date	Type of Marks
EB&CO	Erastus Barton & Co.	New York, N.Y.	fl. 1820's	Oblong punch
E-C	Elias Camp	Bridgeport, Conn.	About 1825	Oblong punch-serrated edges
EC	Ebenezer Chittenden	New Haven, Conn.	1726-1812	Oblong or oval punch
EH	Eliphaz Hart	Norwich, Conn.	1789-1866	Oblong punch
EL	Edward Lang	Salem, Mass.	1742-1830	Oblong punch
EME	Edgar M. Eoff	New York, N.Y.	1785-1858	Oblong punch
EP.	Edward Pear	Boston, Mass.	fl. 1830's	Oblong punch-serrated edges
EP	Elias Pelletreau	Southampton, N.Y.	1726-1810	Oblong punch
EPL	Edward P. Lescure	Philadelphia, Pa.	fl. 1820's	Oblong punch with italic caps
E&P	Eoff & Phyfe	New York, N.Y.	About 1844	Oblong punch, P forms round end
E&S	Easton & Sanford	Nantucket, Mass.	About 1816	Oblong punch
F.&G.	Fletcher & Gardiner	Philadelphia, Pa.	About 1812	Oblong punch
F&H	Farrington & Hunnewell	Boston, Mass.	fl. 1830's	Oblong punch
F.M.	Frederick Marquand	New York, N.Y.	fl. 1820's	Oblong punch, also F-M
F&M	Frost & Munford	Providence, R.I.	About 1810	Oblong punch-serrated edges
F.W.C.	Francis W. Cooper	New York, N.Y.	fl. 1840's	Small oblong punch with FWC over NY
GB or G.B.	Geradus Boyce	New York, N.Y.	About 1814	Oblong punch
GC	George Canon	Warwick, R.I.	Early 1800's	Oblong punch
G&D	Goodwin & Dodd	Hartford, Conn.	Circa, 1813	Oblong punch
G&H	Gale & Hayden	New York, N.Y.	fl. 1840's	Oblong punch-tilted corners
G&M	Gale & Moseley	New York, N.Y.	About 1830	Oblong punch with serrated or plain edges
GRD	G.R. Downing	New York, N.Y.	Circa, 1810	Oblong punch

SELECTED AMERICAN SILVERSMITHS MARKS
1800-1900

Mark	Silversmith	City & State	Date	Type of Marks
G&S	Gale & Stickler	New York, N.Y.	fl. 1820's	Oblong punch
G.W.&H	Gale, Wood & Hughes	New York, N.Y.	About 1835	Oblong punch with serrated or plain edges
H&B	Hart & Brewer	Middletown, Conn.	Early 1800's	Oblong punch
H&H	Hall & Hewson	Albany, N.Y.	About 1819	Oblong punch
H&I	Heydorn & Imlay	Hartford, Conn.	Circa, 1810	Oblong punch- waved edges
H.L	Harvey Lewis	Philadelphia, Pa.	About 1811	Oblong punch
H.L.W.&CO	Henry L. Webster & Co.	Providence, R.I.	fl. 1840's	Oblong Punch
H&M	Hall & Merriman	New Haven, Conn.	Circa, 1826	Incised
HP	Henry Pitkin	East Hartford, Conn.	Circa, 1830's	Flattened octagonal punch
HRT	Henry R. Truax	Albany, N.Y.	About 1815	Plain HRT in plain oblong punch
HS	Hezekia Silliman	New Haven, Conn.	1739-1804	Oblong punch
H&S	Hart & Smith	Baltimore, Md.	Circa, 1815	Oblong punch- also H&S incised
H&S	Hotchkiss & Shreuder	Syracuse, N.Y.	Mid 1800's	H in Diamond-shape punch & round punch, S in round punch
H&W	Hart & Wilcox	Norwich, Conn.	Early 1800's	Oblong punch
IA	I. Adam	Alexandria, Va.	Circa, 1800	Oval punch, italic caps
I-C	Joseph Carpenter	Norwich, Conn.	1747-1804	Oblong punch
I.C or IC	John Coburn	Boston, Mass.	1725-1803	Square punch
IHL	Josiah H. Lownes	Philadelphia, Pa.	Circa, 1822	JHL in oblong punch
I-I	Joseph Jennings	Norwalk, Conn.	1739-1817	Oblong punch
IK	Joseph Keeler	Norwalk, Conn.	1786-1824	Plain or serrated edges, oblong punch
IL or I-L	John Lynch	Baltimore, Md.	1761-1848	Square punch
I-P	Joseph Perkins	Newburyport, Mass.	1766-1849	Crowned IP in shaped scutcheon punch

SELECTED AMERICAN SILVERSMITHS MARKS
1800-1900

Mark	Silversmith	City & State	Date	Type of Marks
I.P.T. & SON	John P. Trott & Son	New London, Conn.	fl. 1820's	Oblong punch
I&PT	John & Peter Targee	New York, N.Y.	Early 1800's	Oblong punch
I-R	Joseph Rogers	Newport, R.I.	About 1808	Flattened oval punch
IR&S	Isaac Reed & Son	Stamford, Conn.	Circa, 1810	Oblong punch
IW	Joshua Weaver	West Chester, Pa.	Circa, 1815	Shaped oval punch
IWF	John W. Forbes	New York, N.Y.	About 1805	IWF over NY-oblong punch
J&A.S	J.&A. Simmons	New York, N.Y.	Early 1800's	Oblong punch
J.B	John Boyce	New York, N.Y.	Circa, 1800	Oblong punch-found with NY in separate Oblong punch
J.B	James Black	Philadelphia, Pa.	About 1811	Oblong punch
J.C.M.	John C. Moore	New York, N.Y.	fl. 1840's	Oblong punch
J.F	Foster & Richards	New York, N.Y.	About 1815	Oblong punch
J.H.C	John H. Connor	New York, N.Y.	fl. 1830's	Oblong punch
J.L.W	John L. Westervell	Newburgh, N.Y.	About 1845	Oblong punch
JM	J. Merchant	New York, N.Y.	Circa, 1860-80	Oval punch
J.P.W.	Joseph P. Warner	Baltimore, Md.	1811-1862	Oblong punch
JS	Joel Sayre	New York, N.Y.	1778-1818	Oblong punch
J.S.B	John Starr Blackman	Danbury, Conn.	1777-1851	Flattened oval or oblong punch
JW	James Ward	Hartford, Conn.	1768-1856	Oval punch
J.W.B	Joseph W. Boyd	New York, N.Y.	Circa, 1820	Oblong punch
J.W.F.	John W. Faulkner	New York, N.Y.	Circa, 1835	Oblong punch
J&W	Jones & Ward	Boston, Mass.	Mid 1800's	Oval punch
K.C.&J.	Kidney, Cann & Johnson	New York, N.Y.	Mid 1800's	Oblong punch
K&D	Kidney & Dunn	New York, N.Y.	fl. 1840's	Oblong punch-plain or serrated edges
K.&S.	Kirk & Smith	Baltimore, Md.	Circa, 1815	Oblong punch

SELECTED AMERICAN SILVERSMITHS MARKS
1800-1900

Mark	Silversmith	City & State	Date	Type of Marks
L.B	Luther Bradley	New Haven, Conn.	1772-1830	Oblong punch
L&G	Lincoln & Green	Boston, Mass.	Circa, 1810	Oblong punch
LH	Littleton Holland	Baltimore, Md.	1770-1847	Oblong punch-italic caps
L&W	Leonard & Wilson	Philadelphia, Pa.	About 1847	Oblong punch-serrated edges
MB	Miles Beach	Litchfield, Conn.	1743-1828	M-B in oblong punch or rounded oval punch
M&B	Merriman & Bradley	New Haven, Conn.	About 1817	Oblong punch-Plain or serrated edges
M.G or MG	Miles Gorham	New Haven, Conn.	1757-1847	Oblong punch
M.J or MJ	Munson Jarvis	Stamford, Conn.	1742-1824	Oblong punch
MM	Marcus Merriman	New Haven, Conn.	1762-1850	M-M in oblong punch-M in square punch-MM in separaet punch
M.M&Co	Marcus Merriman & Co.	New Haven, Conn.	About 1817	Oblong punch-serrated edges
MP or M-P	Matthew Petit	New York, N.Y.	About 1811	Oblong punch
N-A	Nathaniel Austin	Boston, Mass.	1734-1818	Oblong punch
NH	Nicholas Hutchins	Baltimore, Md.	1777-1845	Flattened oval punch
N.H&CO	N. Harding & Co.	Boston, Mass.	Circa, 1830	Oblong punch
NS	Nathaniel Shipman	Norwich, Conn.	1764-1853	Oblong punch
NV	Nathaniel Vernon	Charleston, S.C.	1777-1843	Oblong punch
O&S	Oakes & Spencer	Hartford, Conn.	Circa, 1814	Oblong punch
PDR	Peter De Riemer	Philadelphia, Pa.	1736-1814	Oblong punch-also with rounded ends
P.L.	Peter Lupp	New Brunswick, N.J.	1797-1827	Oval punch
P.L.K	Peter L. Krider	Philadelphia, Pa.	Mid 1800's	Oblong punch
P.M	P. Mood	Charleston, S.C.	About 1806	Oblong punch
PR	Paul Revere II	Boston, Mass.	1735-1818	PR in italic caps-circle or oblong punch

SELECTED AMERICAN SILVERSMITHS MARKS
1800-1900

Mark	Silversmith	City & State	Date	Type of Marks
P.S	Philip Sadtler	Baltimore, Md.	1771-1860	Shaped oblong punch
P&U	Pelletreau & Upson	New York, N.Y.	About 1818	Oblong punch
R.&A.C.	R.&A. Campbell	Baltimore, Md.	About 1853	Oblong punch
RB	Roswell Bartholomew	Hartford, Conn.	1781-1830	Oblong punch-serrated edges
RC	Robert Campbell	Baltimore, Md.	About 1834	Oblong punch
RE or R-E	Robert Evans	Boston, Mass.	1812	Oblong punch
R&G	Riggs & Griffith	Baltimore, Md.	About 1816	Oblong punch
R-M	Reuben Merriman	Litchfield, Conn.	1783-1866	Oblong punch-serrated edges
RR	Richard Riggs	Philadelphia, Pa.	1819	Shaped oval oblong punch
RW or R-W	Robert Wilson	New York, N.Y.	About 1816	Oval punch
R&WW	R.&W. Wilson	Philadelphia, Pa.	fl. 1820's	Oblong punch
SA	Samuel Avery	Preston, Conn.	1760-1836	Oblong punch-also with SA in italic caps
SB	Standish Barry	Baltimore, Md.	1763-1844	Oblong punch
SB	Samuel Buel	Middletown, Conn.	1742-1819	S-B in oblong punch-also rounded oval punch
S&B	Shepherd & Boyd	Albany, N.Y.	About 1810	Oblong punch
SC&Co	Simon Chaudrons & Co.	Philadelphia, Pa.	About 1807	Oblong punch
S&C	Storrs & Cooley	New York, N.Y.	Circa, 1830	Shaped punch
S*D	Samuel Drowne	Portsmouth, N.H.	1749-1815	Flattened oval punch
SH or S-H	Stephen Hardy	Portsmouth, N.H.	1781-1843	Oblong punch
S.K	Samuel Kirk	Baltimore, Md.	1792-1872	Oblong punch-plain or serrated edges
S-M	Samuel Merriman	New Haven, Conn.	1769-1805	Oblong punch
S&M	Sibley & Marble	New Haven, Conn.	1801-1806	Oblong punch

SELECTED AMERICAN SILVERSMITHS MARKS
1800-1900

Mark	Silversmith	City & State	Date	Type of Marks
S&R	Sayre & Richards	New York, N.Y.	About 1802	Flattened oval or oblong punch
SS	Silas Sawin	Boston, Mass.	About 1823	Square punch
TA	Thomas Arnold	Newport, R.I.	1739-1828	Oblong punch-Roman or italic caps
TB	Timothy Brigden	Albany, N.Y.	About 1813	Oblong punch-serrated edges
T-B	Thomas Burger	New York, N.Y.	Circa, 1805	Oblong punch
TC	Thomas Carson	Albany, N.Y.	Circa, 1815	Shaped punch
T.C.C.	Thomas Chester Coit	Norwich, Conn.	Circa, 1812	Oblong punch
T.C&H	Thomas Carson & Hall	Albany, N.Y.	About 1818	Oblong punch
T.E.	Thomas Knox Emery	Boston, Mass.	1781-1815	Oblong punch
T.E.S	T.E. Stebbins	New York, N.Y.	About 1810	Oblong punch
T&H	Taylor & Hinsdale	New York, N.Y.	About 1810	Oblong punch
T-K	Thomas Kinne	Norwich, Conn.	1786-1824	TK and T.K. in oblong punches
T.K.	Thaddeus Keeler	New York, N.Y.	About 1805	Oblong punch
TN	Thomas Norton	Farmington, Conn.	1796-1806	Oblong punch
T.W	Thomas H. Warner	Baltimore, Md.	1780-1828	Shaped oval punch
T-W	Thomas Whartenby	Philadelphia, Pa.	About 1811	Oblong punch
U&B	Ufford & Burdick	New Haven, Conn.	Circa, 1814	Oblong punch
V&W	VanNess & Waterman	New York, N.Y.	About 1835	Oblong punch
W&B	Ward & Bartholomew	Hartford, Conn.	About 1804	Oblong punch
W.B.N.	William B. North	New York, N.Y.	1787-1838	Oblong punch
W&B	Ward & Bartholomew	Hartford, Conn.	About 1804	Oblong punch-plain or serrated edges

SELECTED AMERICAN SILVERSMITHS MARKS
1800-1900

Mark	Silversmith	City & State	Date	Type of Marks
W-C	William Cleveland	New London, Conn.	1770-1837	WC in oblong punch-
W-F	William Forbes	New York, N.Y.	About 1830	Oblong punch
WG	William Gale	New York, N.Y.	About 1816	Oblong punch
W.G.	William Gurley	Norwich, Conn.	Early 1800's	Oblong punch
W&G	Woodward & Grosjean	Boston, Mass.	About 1847	Oblong punch-rounded ends
W.G&S	William Gale & Son	New York, N.Y.	About 1823	Oblong punch
W.H.	William Homes, Jr.	New York, N.Y.	1742-1835	Oblong punch-also WH
W&H	Wood & Hughes	New York, N.Y.	About 1846	Oblong punch
WJ	William B. Johonnot	Middletown, Conn.	1766-1849	Oblong punch
WM	William Moulton	Newburyport, Mass.	Circa, 1807	Oblong punch
W-R	William Roe	Kingston, N.Y.	Early 1800's	Oblong punch
W-S	William Simes	Portsmouth, N.H.	1773-1824	Oblong punch-rounded corners
W-S-N	William S. Nichol	Newport, R.I.	1785-1871	Oblong punch
W.S.P. with TR	Pelletreau & Richards	New York, N.Y.	Circa, 1825	Separate oblong punches
W.S.P.	William Smith Pelletreau	Southampton, L.I., N.Y.	1786-1842	Oblong punch-serrated edges
W.W.	William Ward	Litchfield, Conn.	1742-1828	Oblong punch
WWG	W.W. Gaskins	Providence, R.I.	1830's	Oblong punch
ZS	Zebulon Smith	Maine	1786-1865	

USEFUL PERIODICALS

AMERICAN COLLECTOR (CL)
    13920 Mt. McClellan Blvd., Reno, Nevada 89506

ANTIQUES JOURNAL (CL)
    P.O. Box 1046, Dubuque, Iowa 52001

ANTIQUES MAGAZINE (CL)
    Box N. 467, Kewanee, Illinois 61443

ANTIQUES MAGAZINE (CL)
    551 Fifth Avenue, New York, N.Y. 10017

ANTIQUE TRADER WEEKLY (CL)
    P.O. Box 1050, Dubuque, Iowa 52001

COLLECTOR EDITIONS (Incorporating Acquire) CL
    170 Fifth Avenue, New York, N.Y. 10010

COLLECTORS WEEKLY (CL)
    Drawer C, Kermit, Texas 79745

CONNOISSEUR MAGAZINE (CL)
    250 W. 55th St., New York, N.Y. 10019

SILVER MAGAZINE (CL)
    1619-A SW Jefferson Street, Portland, Oregon 97201

SOTHEBY-PARKE BERNET AUCTION CATALOGS
    980 Madison Avenue, New York, N.Y. 10021

SPINNING WHEEL MAGAZINE (CL)
    Exchange Pl., Hanover, Pennsylvania 17331

RECOMMENDED READING

On the following pages is a listing of recommended reading for beginning silver collectors compiled for the American Silver Collectors Society.

This comprehensive list was provided to the Society by Dorothy T. Rainwater and is reprinted here with her permission.

It is strongly recommended that anyone interested in silver and silverplate join the Society. The address and membership schedule is printed below:

Associate Member $7.50. Additional family member, $1.00 each.

Active Member $5.00. Additional family member, $3.00 each.

        AMERICAN SILVER COLLECTORS SOCIETY
        6213 Joyce Drive
        Washington, D.C. 20031

American Silver

Fales, Martha. *Early American Silver for the Cautious Collector.* Funk & Wagnalls, 1970.

Flynt, Henry N. & Fales, Martha Gandy. *The Heritage Collection of Silver, Old Deerfield, Massachusetts.* Heritage Foundation, 1968.

Hood, Graham. *American Silver, A History of Style, 1659-1900.* Praeger Publishers, 1971.

Kovel, Ralph M. & Terry H. *American Silver, Pewter & Silverplate.* Crown Publishers, 1961.

McClinton, Katherine Morrison. *Collecting American 19th Century Silver.* Charles Scribner's Sons, 1968.

Rainwater, Dorothy T. *Encyclopedia of American Silver Manufacturers.* Everybodys Press, 1975.

Rainwater, Dorothy T. & H. Ivan. *American Silverplate.* Everybodys Press, 1972.

Rainwater, Dorothy T. *Sterling Silver Holloware.* Pyne Press, 1973.

Turner, Noel D. *American Silver Flatware, 1837-1910.* A. S. Barnes, 1972.

American Silver Regional

Beckman, E. D. *Cincinnati Silversmiths, Jewelers, Watch & Clockmakers.* B. & B. Co., Cincinnati, 1975.

Bohan, Peter & Hammerslough, Philip. *Early Connecticut Silver, 1700-1840.* Wesleyan University Press, 1970.

Burton, E. Milby. *South Carolina Silversmiths, 1690-1860.* Charleston Museum, 1968.

Carlisle, Lilian Baker. *Vermont Clock and Watchmakers, Silversmiths and Jewelers, 1778-1878.* Burlington, Vermont, 1970.

Currier, Ernest M. *Marks of Early American Silversmiths.* Reprinted 1970 by Robert Alan Green.

Cutten, George Barton. *Silversmiths of Georgia.* Pigeonhold Press, 1958.

Cutten, George Barton. *Silversmiths of North Carolina.* State Dept. of Archives & History, 1948.

Cutten, George Barton. *Silversmiths of Virginia.* Dietz Press, reprinted 1976.

Gerstell, Vivian S. *Silversmiths of Lancaster, Pennsylvania 1730-1850.* Lancaster County Historical Society, 1972.

Hiatt, Noble W. and Lucy F. *The Silversmiths of Kentucky.* Standard Printing Co., 1954.

Hoitsma, Muriel Cutten. *Early Cleveland Silversmiths.* Gates Publishing Co., 1953.

Knittle, Rhea Mansfield. *Early Ohio Silversmiths and Pewterers 1787-1847.* Calvert-Hatch Co., 1943.

Maryland Silver in the Collection of the Baltimore Museum of Art (18th & 19th century) Baltimore Museum of Art, 1975.

New York State Silversmiths. Darling Foundation. 1965. (RARE)

Pleasants, J. Hall and Sill, Howard. *Maryland Silversmiths, 1715-1830.* Reprinted in 1972 by Robert Alan Green.

Roach, Ruth Hunter. *St. Louis Silversmiths.* Privately printed, 1967.

Williams, Carl M. *Silversmiths of New Jersey, 1700-1825*. G. S. McManus Co., 1949.

Fredyma, John J. *Directory of Connecticut Silversmiths & Watch and Clock Makers*. 1973.

Fredyma, James P. *Directory of Maine Silversmiths & Watch and Clock Makers*. 1972.

Fredyma, P. J. & M. L. *Directory of Massachusetts Silversmiths*. 1972.

Fredyma, P. J. & M. L. *Directory of New Hampshire Silversmiths*. 1971.

Fredyma, P. J. & M. L. *Directory of Rhode Island Silversmiths*. 1972.

(Available from Marie-Louise Fredyma, Hanover, New Hampshire 03755)

Foreign Silver

Albrecht, Kurt. *Nineteenth Century Australian Gold & Silversmiths*. Hutchinson Group, Australia, 1969.

Hawkins, J. B. *Australian Silver, 1800-1900*. National Trust of Australia, 1973. (Both books on Australian silver available from Robert Alan Green)

Langdon, John Emerson. *Canadian Silversmiths & Their Marks, 1667-1867*. Stinehour Press, 1960.

Bøje, Chr. A. Dansk Guld Og Sølv. *Smedemaerker For 1870*. (Silversmiths' marks) Politikens Forlag, 1954.

Boesen, Gudmund and Bøje, Dhr. A. *Old Danish Silver*. Hassing Publisher, 1959.

Gans, M. H. and de Wit-Klinkhamer, Th. M. Duyvene. *Dutch Silver*. Faber & Faber, 1958.

Bradbury, Frederick. *History of Old Sheffield Plate*. Northend Publishers, reprinted 1968.

Fallon, John P. *The Marks of the London Goldsmiths and Silversmiths, Georgian Period* (c. 1697-1837) David & Charles Publishers, 1972.

Grimwade, Arthur G. *London Goldsmiths, 1697-1837, Their Marks & Lives*. Faber & Faber, 1975.

Jackson, Sir Charles J. *An Illustrated History of English Plate*. 2 vols. Dover reprint, 1969.

Jackson, Sir Charles J. *English Goldsmiths and Their Marks*. Dover reprint, 1964.

Snodin, Michael. *English Silver Spoons*. Charles Letts & Co., 1974.

Dennis, Faith. *Three Centuries of French Domestic Silver*. 2 vols. Metropolitan Museum of Art, 1960.

French Master Goldsmiths and Silversmiths, 17th to 19th Century. French & European Publications, Inc., 1966.

Strong, D. C. *Greek and Roman Gold and Silver Plate*. Cornell University Press 1966

Andren, Erik. *Swedish Silver*. M. Barrows & Co., 1950.

Brunner, Herbert. *Old Table Silver*. Taplinger Publishing Co., 1964.

Emery, John. *European Spoons Before 1700*. John Donald Publishers, 1976.

Forbes, H. A. Crosby; Kernan, John Devereux and Wilkins, Ruth S. *Chinese Export Silver, 1785-1885*. Museum of the American China Trade, 1975.

Hughes, Graham. *Modern Silver Throughout the World, 1880-1967*. Crown Publishers, 1967.

Link, Eva M. *The Book of Silver*. Praeger Publishers, 1973.

Les Poincons de Garantie Internationaux pour L'Argent. Tardy Publishers, 9th edition.

GLOSSARY

On these pages are found a listing of words and terms used in this book and in addition many others you are likely to encounter in other reading and discussing of silver.

Many of the words and terms are more widely defined as they are used in areas other than silver. The definitions found here are as they apply to silver and silverplate.

Acanthus— A form of ornamentation taken from the leaf of the acanthus plant. Originally used extensively on the Corinthian capital throughout the Renaissance.

Ajoure— A French term applied to metalwork which is perforated, pierced, or open.

Albata— A less commonly used word to describe Nickel Silver or German Silver.

Alchemy— An alloy of tin and copper used to make a very high quality pewter in the 16th and 17th centuries. The word obviously derives from the Dark Ages and Renaissance erroneous attempts to turn base metals into gold.

Alcomy— An alloy of several base metals primarily used in button making.

Alloy— A substance made up of two or more metals usually mixed in molten form.

Alpacca— A less common synonym of Nickel Silver or German silver.

Aluminum Silver— A composition of aluminum and silver, usually 3 parts silver to 97 parts aluminum. The resulting alloy is considerably harder than aluminum.

Amorini— A silver decoration consisting of cupids or cherubs. Italian in origin.

Amphora— A vase or container with an ovoid shaped body, short neck and two loop handles, one on either side.

Anneal— A process by which silver is repeatedly reheated after gradual cooling to keep it malleable while it is being worked. It has the added advantage of removing or reducing internal stress in the object being fashioned.

Anthemion— Honeysuckle motif in decoration imspired from classical architecture, often found on Sheffield Plate.

Applied Work— Details (spouts, handles, etc.) and decoration which have been made separately and applied to the object with solder.

Arabesque— A complex interwoven design from the Italian Renaissance period.

Argentine— An alloy of tin and antimony used as a base for silver plating. Sometimes used synonymously with Nickel Silver or German Silver.

Argyle— A container for serving sauces, made with an inner jacket to hold hot water for the purpose of maintaining heat. Originally manufactured in silver but found made of glass in contemporary pieces.

Assay— A test to determine whether a metal is of the required quality.

Base Metal— An alloy or metal of relatively low value to which a coating or plating is applied.

Beading— A border ornament composed of small beadlike contiguous protrusions. Commonly found on silver of the later 18th and early 19th centuries.

Bell Metal— A type of old Sheffield Plate consisting of a very heavy coating of silver. First produced in 1789.

Bleeding— Technical term pertaining to pieces of silverplate where the copper base is exposed.

Bobeche— Flat or saucer-shaped dish placed around a candle base to catch wax drippings.

Bright-cut— A form of engraved decoration whereupon a portion of the metal is removed with a sharp bevelled cutting instrument. The result is a jewel-like faceted sparkle on the surface.

Bright Finish— Highly polished surface obtained by using jeweler's rouge on a polishing wheel.

Britannia— An alloy closely related to pewter but differing in composition. It is made up of tin, copper and antimony as is pewter, but contains no lead as does most old pewter. It was frequently used as a base metal in the early days of the silver plating industry.

Bronze— An alloy mostly composed of copper and tin.

Buffing— Polishing the surface of metal, usually with a flexible mechanical wheel, thereby removing a thin outer layer of metal, leaving a smooth mar-free surface.

Burnishing— When silverplate is formed it is composed of crystalline forms aggregated upon the surface of the base metal. A hard tool is used to rub the surface to smooth and harden the silverplate by spreading the crystals together and forcing them into the surface irregularities of the base metal. The result is a harder, more durable finish which is twice as resistant to tarnishing.

Butler Finish— The surface appearance obtained by buffing with a wire wheel. The wheel imparts countless tiny scratches to the surface, resulting in a dull appearance.

C.— See Coin

Cable— An ornament similar to twisted rope. Derived from Norman architecture.

Cafe au lait Pots— Refers to a pair of side handled coffee dispensers from which hot milk and coffee are poured at the same time.

Cann— A lidless, one handled drinking vessel.

Cartouche— A motif in the shape of a shield or scroll with curled edges.

Caryatid— A statue of a woman used as a column or base.

Cast— Formed in a mold. Examples: handles and ornaments to be applied to an object.

Caudle Cup— A large two-handled bowl that was used for serving a wine-flavored gruel known as "caudle".

Chafing Dish— A dish within a dish, supported by a stand in which is a heat source. The outer dish, in direct contact with the heat, is filled with water with the inner dish containing food.

Chamberstick/Chamber-candlestick— A short candle holder consisting of a saucer the center of which is a candle holder and bears a ring on the perimeter for ease of carrying. Was used for finding one's way after all the lamps in the house were extinguished for the night.

Champleve— Grooves or troughs are cut into the metal surface and filled with enamel ingredients. These are then melted. The surface is then usually ground smooth, then polished.

Chasing— (see flat-chasing and repousse). A vague general term used to describe effects produced by using chisels and hammers on cold metal without the removal of any of the metal.

Ciborium— A goblet shaped container used in religious services to contain the Eucharistic wafers.

Cloissone— A design is applied to the surface of the object by means of soldering a wire or metal ribbon on edge in the desired design. The enamel is then poured into the network of cells fused and then ground and polished. The result is a beautiful enamel design with the wire or ribbon edges showing through.

Coin/Coin Silver— Term used to indicate 900 parts of silver and 100 parts of copper in 1000 parts. This is the standard used in United States silver coins. Used by Colonial U.S. silversmiths who had no sterling available. Also C.D., Pure Coin, Dollar, Standard or Premium.

Commercial Silver— 999/1000 fine or higher.

Craig Silver— Used in making knives. Similar to German Silver.

C-Scroll/Single Scroll— A Rococo scroll design in the form of the letter "C" applied to the shape of a handle.

Cutler— One who deals in, sells, makes, or repairs knives and cooking and eating utensils.

Cutlery— Knives having a cutting edge.

Date Letters— The insigne given by the London Goldsmiths Company to signify the year of manufacture of the piece of silver.

Dish Cross— A silver or silverplate article used to support a bowl or dish ring. Sometimes has an alcohol lamp for warming contents.

Dish Ring— A round pierced holder for wooden or porcelain bowl. Sometimes known as a potato ring. Irish origin.

Dolphin— Motif utilizing the sea dolphin.

Domed— Spheroid type of cover, first used in the early 18th Century on tankards, teapots and coffee pots.

Domestic Plate— Silverplated ware used in the home.

Double-scroll— A line in an S-shape. Reverse curves used in the design of handles.

Draw Plates— Metal parts of a drawing bench (hole dies) through which wire is drawn to reduce its size or change its shape.

Electrolysis— The process of conducting an electric current by an electrolyte of charged particles. This process is used to remove silver in stripping or to deposit silver on a base metal to form silverplate.

Electroplate (see electrolysis)— Refers to articles made of a base metal coated with silver utilizing the process of electrolysis.

Electrotype— Reproduction of an art object by electroplating a wax impression.

Electrum— A natural pale yellow alloy of gold and silver. Also an imitative alloy of silver made up of 8 parts copper, 4 parts nickel and 3½ parts zinc.

Embossing— Making raised designs on the surface of an object by hammering from the reverse side. See repousse.

Engraving— Forming a design decoration on the metal by removing or cutting away the metal.

EPBM— Electroplate on Britannia metal.

EPC— Electroplate on Copper.

Epergne— An elaborate assemblage of containers around a larger center dish, all held by a metal stand of some sort. Used primarily as a table centerpiece.

EPNS— Electroplate on Nickel Silver.

EPNS-WMM— Electroplate on Nickel Silver with White Metal "mounts" (handles, spouts, finials, feet, borders, etc.)

EPWM— Electroplate on White Metal.

Etching— A surface decoration bitten in with acid.

Ewer— A pitcher or jug with a handle and wide spout.

Feather Edge— A chased edge of slanting lines. Usually used to ornament spoon handles.

Festoon— A garland of leaves or flowers hanging in a curve.

Fine Pewter— A term applied to a composition having a smooth surface, attractive color and strength which is used primarily for plate-making. It is composed of 20% brass or copper and 80% tin.

Fine Silver— A term applied to silver which is more than 999/1000 pure. Too soft for most purposes, it is used as the plate or anode (source of silver) in the electroplating process.

Finial— A crowing or terminating ornament on covers, often in figural form; animals or flowers, etc.

Flagon — Large container used for serving wine, ale or other liquors.

Flame — A term referring to a removable decoration used in place of a candle. Usually found in the center of candelabrum.

Flash Plate — Unbuffed, cheap plated ware.

Flat Chasing — Surface decoration in very low relief. Popular in England in the early 1700's and most popular in late 18th Century and all through 19th Century America also.

Flatware — Most often refers to silver knives, forks, spoons and serving pieces. Also can be used to describe plates, platters and other flat pieces, though not commonly used so.

Flutting — A type of grooving generally associated with wide, smooth concave (turned in) grooves with ridges between.

Fly Spoon — A spoon, with a cut-out design in the bowl, used to remove flies or specks of dirt from wine in a chalice.

Forging — Usually refers to the fashioning of metal into forms by alternate heating and hammering. It is not technically necessary to apply heat to form by forcing.

Fusion — Process of melting, as in the fusion of metals. Usually accomplished with the application of intense heat.

Gadroon — A border ornament of reeds and flutes, usually in a spiral. Sometimes referred to as Knurling.

Geometric — An angled line design.

Gilding — Prior to the introduction of electroplating, the usual method of coating a metal with silver or gold was to mix it with Mercury, apply it to the object and heat it. This evaporated the Mercury, leaving the silver or gold lay on the object.

German Silver — (see Nickel Silver).

Gold Plating — Covering an object with a layer of gold by electroplating or gilding.

Goldsmiths' Company — The organization under whose jurisdiction falls the regulation of the English silver industry.

Graver — A type of chisel used in the engraving of silver.

Guilloche — A decorative motif of interlaced circular forms, usually having a flower in the center.

Hallmark — The official mark used by the London Goldsmiths' Company on articles of gold and silver to indicate their genuineness.

Hollow Handle (H.H.) — Handle made by joining two halves by soldering. About 35 years ago International Silver Company developed a process to produce one piece seamless hollow handles. This process is used to fashion much of the better quality hollow handle pieces now.

61

Hollow Ware— A general term applying to objects in the form of hollow vessels such as bowls, pitchers, pots, and mugs. Anything other than knives, forks, spoons and serving pieces. (Flatware)

Husks— Festoons of seeds.

Imperial Measure— Legal standard weights and measures used in England.

Ingot— Bar of silver or other metal.

King's Head— A mark on a piece of silver indicating payment of a tax assessed by the Crown.

Latten— An alloy of copper, zinc and brass.

Limoges— Enamel covering the surface of metal.

London Goldsmiths' Company— (see Goldsmiths' Company).

Maker's Mark— A mark, initials, etc. struck on a piece of silver usually indicating who made it.

Malleable— Capable of being extended or molded by beating with a hammer.

Marrow Scoop— A long, thin silver utensil used for extracting marrow from bone.

Matte Finish (Matted ground)— A dull surface finish produced by light hammering or punch work; to contrast it with a burnished surface.

Metalsmith— One who works in metal.

Monteith— A large bowl with a deeply notched rim. Used for chilling glasses.

Motif— A prominent feature in the makeup or design of a work.

Mounts— Handles, spouts, finials, feet, borders, etc.

Nickel Silver (German Silver)— An alloy of nickle, copper and zinc; usually 65 percent copper, 5 to 25 percent nickel, and 10 to 30 percent zinc.

Niello— Line engraving on gold or silver which is filled in with a type of black enamel.

Non-tarnishing Silver— Used mostly for jewelry; produced either by alloying silver with cadmium or by the application of a thin plating of rhodium or palladium to the surface.

Nozzle— A socket for a candlestick.

N.S.— Nickel Silver.

Ormolu— Group-up gold leaf used as a pigment for gilding. Can be brass made to look like gold.

Oxidizing— Application of an oxide to a metal to darken the surface. Used to heighten detail by emphasizing shadows and highlights, creating a look of depth.

Parcel-gilt— Seldom used old fashioned term meaning "partly gilt".

Patina— Soft luster; the appearance of a metal surface usually naturally achieved by the use of age.

Peg Tankard— A vessel with measuring notches inside; used to hold ale or beer.

Pewter — Commonly, a metal alloy composed of tin, copper and usually lead. The higher the tin content, the better the pewter. Pewter produced today does not contain lead.

Piercing — Openwork decoration.

Pipkin — A container, usually with handle extending at right angles, used for sauces.

Planishing — To make smooth. To smooth the hammer marks left in fashioning a silver piece by the use of a flat-faced, oval shaped hammer called a planishing hammer.

Plate — A term used in England and other parts of Europe to describe objects made of a solid precious metal. Not to be confused with the term silverplate widely used in the United States to describe objects plated with silver by electroplating process.

Plateau — A rectangular, oval, or circular centerpiece consisting of a flat mirror framed in metal.

Plique-a-jour — Translucent enamel without a backing, framed within metalwork. The effect is much like that of stained glass.

Pricking — Delicate engraving using a needle point instrument.

Pure Coin — (see Coin)

Raising — Creation of a piece of hollow ware from a flat sheet of metal by hammering in ever-increasing concentric circles over a series of anvils.

Repousse — A refinement of embossing wherein a raised design is hammered out from the inside of an object and then usually enhanced by surface chasing.

Reticulated — Piercing on the rims or sides of hollow ware.

Revolving Tureen — Vessel with a roll cover and hot water compartment, originally used during the Victorian Era.

Rococo — An extremely ornate, curvilinear form of decoration imitative of foliage, scrolls and shellwork. Originated in France during the reign of Louis XV.

Rolled Plate (R.P.) — see Sheffield Plate.

Rope Molding — A border design, slightly spiraled and resembling a rope.

Satin Finish — Satin Finish is produced by the same process as Butler Finish, but leaves relatively deep scratches in the object while Butler Finish is simply on the surface.

Scorper — Small, variously shaped chisels used in engraving.

Scroll — A spiralled ornamentation.

Serrated — Toothed or notched.

Sheffield Plate (see page 9-10) — Frequently called "Old Sheffield Plate" to distinguish it from electroplate. Developed around 1743 by Thomas Boulsover, a sheet of copper is fused with a thin sheet of silver on one or both sides then the resultant sheet is rolled down to the desired thickness. It was then ready to work.

Silver Edge – A decorative border made of solid silver.

Silverplate (Silver Plate) – A term commonly used to describe articles made of a base metal and then electroplated with silver. Not to be confused with "Plate" as used in England when referring to solid silver articles.

Silver Shield – The placing of a solid or sterling silver shield device on a piece of plated ware to hold the engraving.

Snuffer – A flame extinguisher.

Soy Stand – A cruet or spice holder.

Spinning – Pressing a flat sheet of metal against a revolving form on a lathe so as to produce a piece of hollow ware.

Stake – An anvil upon which silver objects are found.

Stamping – Using dies and hammers to strike a mark in a piece of metal. Used to decorate.

Standard – (see Coin).

Sterling Silver (see page 8) – 925 parts silver and 75 parts added metal, usually copper, to give silver the needed strength to be worked into durable qualities. It is the standard imposed by the United States government in the Stamping Act of 1906 to assure the quality of the metal.

Stoning – Polishing silver with a special stone made for this purpose.

Strapwork – Narrow, folded interlacing bands or straps.

Swaged – Formed by a process of rolling or hammering.

Syphon Stand – Pierced holder for a seltzer bottle.

Tempering – A process of heating and cooling by which metal is strengthened.

Touch – Silversmith's or maker's mark; impressed with a punch or die.

Touchstone – A hard siliceous stone or modern square of wedgewood on which a piece of silver or gold of known quality can be rubbed to compare its mark with that of a piece being assayed.

Trademark – Symbol or trade name marked on a piece to identify the manufacturer.

Victorian Plate – Silver ware made during the Victorian Era by the process of electrolysis.

Waiter – A service or carrying tray.

White Metal – An alloy made up of two or more of the following: Usually tin withcopper, lead, antimony, or bismuth. The color of the resultant gets whiter as more tin is used.

INTRODUCTION
ENGLISH SILVERSMITHS' MARKS

Although the bulk of this book is devoted to the products of American Silversmiths and Silver & Silverplate manufacturers, an understanding of English Silversmiths' marks, or hallmarks, is important to anyone interested in the subject of Silver.

There are four marks usually stamped or impressed on English silver in the following sequence: The Town, or Hall Mark indicating the location of the assay office; the Date Letter, or Annual Mark indicating when the piece was made; the Makers Mark, the initials of the silversmith in a shaped punch; the Standard, or Sterling Mark indicating Sterling quality.

Other marks found on English Silver are: Brittania Mark (1697 - 1719), required to indicate the higher standard of silver made during that time.

The Duty Mark, or Sovereign's Head (1784-1890) indicating that the duty had been paid on the item marked.

The Jubilee Mark added to pieces dated 1933/4 to 1935/6 to honor the silver Jubilee of King George V. and Queen Mary, and the Coronation mark of 1953 to indicate the acession of Queen Elizabeth II to the throne.

| TOWN MARK | DATE LETTER | MAKERS MARK | STERLING MARK |

ENGLISH SILVER & SILVERPLATE

On the following pages is a representative cross-section of collectible English Silver and Silverplate. The pieces listed are dated from 1623 through 1925. Many of these items are still to be found in antique shops, and at auctions, though they are rising in value and are increasingly scarce. Prices quoted are approximate current retail prices for items in fine condition.

ALL PICTURES ARE FROM THE VICTORIA & ALBERT MUSEUM, LONDON ENGLAND, AND ARE USED WITH PERMISSION.

ENGLISH SILVER & SILVERPLATE

Item, description, date   **Retail**

1. Bedroom candlestick, silver-gilt.
   Maker's mark: Paul de Lamerie. Hallmark: London.
   Circa 1748-9. 5¾″ wide x 3¼″ high......................Set of 4 $3850-4700
2. Candlestick (1 of four), Sheffield plate,
   globe base, round baluster stem, shell ornament
   in relief. English, circa 1830............................Pr. $550.00-875.00
3. Pair of candlesticks, silver, Birmingham hallmark 1906-7,
   maker's mark Liberty & Co...............................Pr. $490.00-740.00
4. Candelabrum (1 of a pair), maker's mark "J.A.,"
   London hallmark 1819-20. 15¾″ high....................$3000.00-3500.00
5. Pair of silver candlesticks, hallmark, Dublin, circa 1704-6......$1750.00-2500.00
6. Candle snuffer and tray, silver. Maker's mark:
   "Thos. Robbins" on snuffer, "John Hawkes" on tray.
   Hallmark: London 1823-4. Tray 9½″ wide.....................$340.00-410.00
7. Card carry case, electroplated silver panel gilt.
   Inscribed "Ellington Mason & Co. 1852,"....................$55.00-75.00
8. Cake basket, silver, Maker's mark "S. Herbert & Co."
   Hallmark "London 1753-4."...............................$2100.00-2440.00
9. Casket, silver set with opals
   Hallmark, Birmingham 1903. Maker's mark, "Liberty & Co."
   Designed by Archibold Knox. Art Nouveau.................$2200.00-2600.00
10. Silver cup, hallmark, London 1623-4.....................$3000.00-3400.00
11. Coffee pot, French sterling silver, Paris 1809-19...............$850.00-1120.00
12. Coffee pot, sterling silver, arms of "stacye,"
    wooden handle, English, Hallmark, London 1753-4...........$1850.00-2100.00
13. Silver coffee pot, maker's mark:
    "David Smith & Robert Sharp," hallmark, London 1765-6.
    10½″ high x 9″ wide.....................................$800.00-1000.00

1.

2.

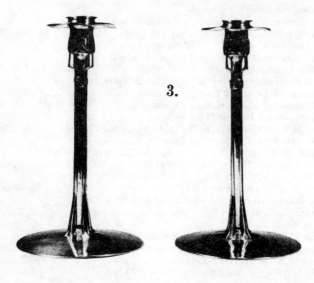

3.

5.

4.

6.

7.

ENGLISH SILVER & SILVERPLATE

8.

9.

10.

11.

ENGLISH SILVER & SILVERPLATE

Item, description, date   **Retail**

14. Cruet stand, silver with glass bottles, maker's mark, "C.C.," hallmark, London 1810-11. 5 7/8″ wide.................................$275.00-300.00

15. Christening cup, silver, designed by "R. Redgrave R.A., " hallmark, London 1865.................$290.00-425.00

16. Cheese dish, mark of "Edward Wakelin," hallmark, London 1760. 14″ wide...........................$785.00-850.00

17. Dish Ring, Silver, English, circa 1730. 10¼″ wide.....................................$540.00-600.00

18. Artichoke dish, silver, hallmark, London 1849-50. ¾″ high, 6½″ deep.........................$390.00-580.00

19. Silver ewer, hallmark, London 1849-9, maker's mark, "Joseph & Albert Savony."............................$700.00-750.00

20. Wine and Spirits labels, silver. English, late 18th and 19th century..............................Set $250.00-310.00

21. Silver wine labels. English, late 18th and 19th century (George III)...............................Set $450.00-500.00

22. Wager cup, silver, maker's mark, "Jas Walker," hallmark, Dublin 1706-8. 6 7/8″ high.....................$1900.00-2100.00

23. Wine cooler, sterling silver, maker's mark, "Frederick Kandler," hallmark, London 1775-6 ..$2000.00-2500.00

23a Candlesticks, silver, maker's mark, "WC," hallmark, London 1771-2........................Pair $1100.00-1400.00

24. Two-handled cup and cover, silver, maker's mark, "James Dixon & Son," hallmark, Sheffield 1850-60............$2230.00-2550.00

25. Two "goats & bee" milk jugs, forged marks, late 19th century, London hallmark. 4½″ high.............Pair $450.00-500.00

26. Inkstand silver, hallmark, London 1845-6, maker's mark, "Robert Hennell.".............................$280.00-390.00

15.

16.

71

17.

18.

19.

20.

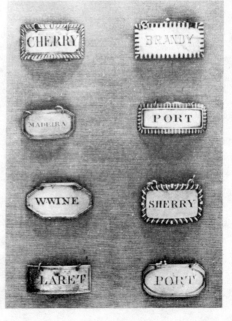

ENGLISH SILVER & SILVERPLATE

22.

21.

23A.

23.

23A.

ENGLISH SILVER & SILVERPLATE

24.

28.

25.

27.

ENGLISH SILVER & SILVERPLATE

Item, description, date	Retail

27. Jug, silver, panel-gilt, hallmark, London 1881-2,
maker's mark, "J. Aldwinkle & James Slater." $315.00-360.00

28. Kettle, stand and spirit burner, silver-plated copper.
Designed by "Arthur Dixon for Birmingham Guild of Handicraft,"
circa 1905-10 .... $390.00-420.00

29. Mug, silver panel-gilt, maker's mark,
"Storr & Mortimer," hallmark, London 1810. 4″ high $200.00-235.00

30. Mug, silver, maker's mark,
"Langlands & Robertson," hallmark, New Castle 1785 .... $225.00-260.00

31. Punch ladle, silver bowl, whatebone handle.
English, 18th century $75.00-85.00

32. Punch ladle, silver, rosewood handle.
Hallmark, London 1731-1 .... $100.00-140.00

33. Stirrup cup, silver, mark of
"W. Barwash & R. Sibley," hallmark, London 1827.
5¾″ high $3500.00-4050.00

34. Silver salver, maker's mark,
"Ja" (John Angell?), hallmark, London 1823-4 .... $1600.00-2000.00

35. Pair of silver sauce bowls, maker's mark,
"B.E." (?), hallmark, London 1751-2
Arms engraved $550.00-760.00

36. *Salt cellar, silver, hallmark, London 1695-6.
2½″ high .... Pr. $775.00-820.00

37. *Salt cellar, silver, English, second half of
the 17th century. 1 1½8″ high .... Pr. $770.00-850.00

38. *Salt cellar, silver, made by "Simon Pantin,"
hallmark, London 1707-8. 2 5/8″ wide .... Pr. 625.00-765.00

39. Silver scone, hallmark, London 1703-4,
engraved maker's mark, "John Rand.' .... Pr. 4900.00-5690.00

ENGLISH SILVER & SILVERPLATE

29.
30.
33.
34.

ENGLISH SILVER & SILVERPLATE

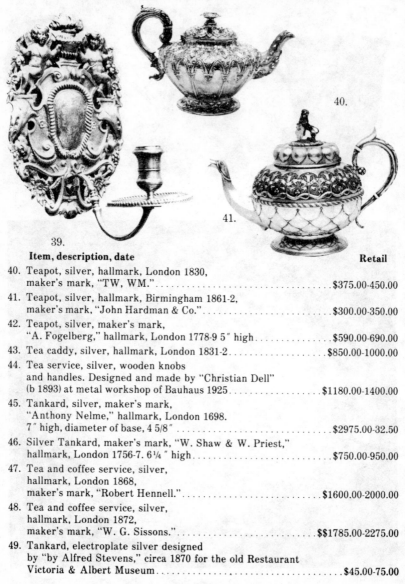

39.

40.

41.

Item, description, date	Retail
40. Teapot, silver, hallmark, London 1830, maker's mark, "TW, WM."	$375.00-450.00
41. Teapot, silver, hallmark, Birmingham 1861-2, maker's mark, "John Hardman & Co."	$300.00-350.00
42. Teapot, silver, maker's mark, "A. Fogelberg," hallmark, London 1778-9 5″ high	$590.00-690.00
43. Tea caddy, silver, hallmark, London 1831-2	$850.00-1000.00
44. Tea service, silver, wooden knobs and handles. Designed and made by "Christian Dell" (b 1893) at metal workshop of Bauhaus 1925	$1180.00-1400.00
45. Tankard, silver, maker's mark, "Anthony Nelme," hallmark, London 1698. 7″ high, diameter of base, 4 5/8″	$2975.00-32.50
46. Silver Tankard, maker's mark, "W. Shaw & W. Priest," hallmark, London 1756-7. 6¼″ high	$750.00-950.00
47. Tea and coffee service, silver, hallmark, London 1868, maker's mark, "Robert Hennell."	$1600.00-2000.00
48. Tea and coffee service, silver, hallmark, London 1872, maker's mark, "W. G. Sissons."	$$1785.00-2275.00
49. Tankard, electroplate silver designed by "by Alfred Stevens," circa 1870 for the old Restaurant Victoria & Albert Museum	$45.00-75.00

ENGLISH SILVER & SILVERPLATE

43.

45.

42.

44.

ENGLISH SILVER & SILVERPLATE

47.

49.

ENGLISH SILVER & SILVERPLATE

46.

48.

AMERICAN SILVER-SILVERPLATE

BAKING DISHES

Inside the baking dish was a porcelain liner in which the item to be baked was placed; this only went into the oven. To serve, the liner was placed on the sterling, or silver plated, receptable.

The baking dish is found with, and without the cover. The most valuable are those complete with original porcelain liners and covers.

Illustrated on these two pages are some typical examples. The current market values shown are entirely dependent on the size, design intricacies, condition and weight of the silver.

Silverplate **$100.00-$225.00**
Sterling Silver **$200.00-$500.00**

Victorian Baking Dish, CIRCA 1880

BAKING DISHES

Prices on preceeding page

BAR ACCESSORIES

A great variety of liquor and bar items were produced from 1860-1900 by American silver and silverplate manufacturers in both sterling silver and silverplate. Corkscrews, muddlers, liquor labels, wine funnels, bar jiggers, bar strainers, glass holders, beer pitchers, hot whiskey pitchers, etc., were made in large quantities and in many designs.

Liquor Labels
Silverplate
$5.00-$20.00
Silver
$15.00-$30.00

BRANDY.

Liquor Label

WHISKEY

Liquor Label

Patent Corkscrew

Jiggers
Silver & Silverplate
$10.00-$30.00

Corkscrews
Silver & Silverplate
$10.00-$100.00

Bar Jigger

Bottle Holder
Silver $40.00-$75.00

Corkscrew

BAR ACCESSORIES

ICE TUBS AND WINE COOLERS

Wine coolers were made during the late 1700's, and were derived from the wine cisterns of the middle 1600's and early 1700's. Cisterns were elaborately embossed large oval bowls, chased with dolphins, mermaids, etc., designed to hold water, ice, and a quantity of wine bottles. They reached very large proportions in the 1700's, often four feet long, and over 1,000 ounces of sterling silver in weight.

Wine coolers which evolved from these cisterns, were made much smaller and more graceful, and held only one bottle of wine. They were usually vase shaped, either footed on a pedestal, or flat, with two handles. The interior was a removeable jacket which held the bottle; the ice was placed between the jacket and outside of the vase. Wine coolers were generally made in pairs, in silver and Sheffield plate in England, and in silver and silverplate in the United States. The designs often featured the grape and leaf motif, although the 1860's and 1900's saw the use of Victorian, rococo, and Art Nouveau designs engraved, inlaid and embossed.

Silverplate—$100.00-220.00
Silver—$300.00-$600.00
Prices depend on size, design &
weight of silver

Ice Tub

Wine Cooler

Ice Tub

BELLS

Among the most popular of small collectibles are bells of all types. Table and call bells were made of glass and china, but the most collected bells are of metal; brass, copper, silver and silverplate.

Table and tea bells of silver and silverplate were made by most American manufacturers in a great variety of designs and shapes, from simple half-round with plain cast handle, to the most elaborate engraved, embossed, and chased examples with figural handles.

Call bells on a base, or legs, have a spring activated clapper that was activated by pressing the button to call a maid or servant. Most are made of silverplate.

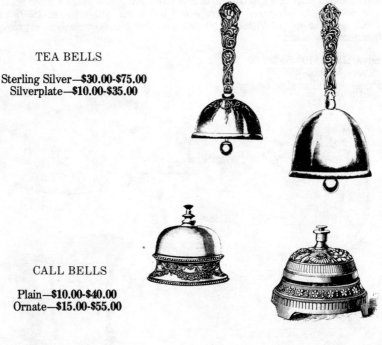

TEA BELLS

Sterling Silver—**$30.00-$75.00**
Silverplate—**$10.00-$35.00**

CALL BELLS

Plain—**$10.00-$40.00**
Ornate—**$15.00-$55.00**

BELLS

Prices on preceeding page

86

BON-BON BASKETS

Bon-bon dishes and baskets were used to serve chocolates and sweets in the late 1890's. The dishes were produced in both sterling silver and silverplate. They were made with elaborate embossed borders, often pierced. Bon-bon baskets featured a variety of embossed, engraved and chased styles, with bail handles, and sometimes with tongs. They are known both footed and flat.

Unger Bros. Silversmith factory of Newark, N.J., made bon-bon dishes in sterling silver in Art Nouveau motifs featuring flowing-haired women and flowers, blossoms, and leaves. These pieces are most desirable and valuable.

Silverplate $30.00-$100.00
*Silver $60.00-$190.00

*Depends on Size & Weight of Silver

BOTTLES & FLASKS—SILVER & GLASS

The combination of Silver, Silverplate and glass of all types reached its zenith during the Victorian and Art Nouveau periods.

Flasks and bottles of all types in cut, pressed, or engraved glass were made in a large variety of designs and patterns, with Sterling or Silverplate tops and often with the bottle seated in a Sterling or Silverplate base, or completely encased in an open fretwork of floral or Rococo design.

This same production technique was used on many colognes and perfume bottles and toilet and atomizer bottles. A blank plaque for engraving initials was usually centered on the fretwork.

Vinaigrettes, or salt bottles, glass puff boxes, inkwells, mucilage bottles and toothbrushes are a part of this highly desirable, valuable and collectable group.

Cut and engraved glass claret jugs with ornate silver handle and pourer, and green-glass brandy decanters encased in floral and rococo design open fretwork silver were popular in the mid 1850's and are sought by both bottle and silver collectors.

A charming and highly collectable type of Victorian and Art Nouveau bottle are the glove colognes. Their slender, tapered shapes enabled them to be worn in the Victorian ladies glove. These miniature cologne receptacles were objects of much decorative art usually with flower motifs, engraved, chased, and embossed on the surface.

See also "Gentlemens Accessories—Pocket Flasks" pg. 172.

BOTTLES & FLASKS, SILVER & GLASS

Silver & Cut Crystal Colognes & Perfume Bottles
$25.00-$75.00 (depends upon size of bottle)

BOTTLES & FLASKS—SILVER & GLASS

Silver & Cut Crystal Liquor Flasks
$45.00-$85.00

Silver Overlay & Crystal Cologne Bottles *$25.00-$65.00

*Price Depends On Size of Bottles

BOTTLES & FLASKS—SILVER & GLASS

Silver Overlay & Crystal Flasks
$25.00-$65.00
Silver Flasks
$75.00-$250.00

Silver & Cut Crystal
Perfume Bottles
$25.00-$75.00

BOXES—SILVER & SILVERPLATE

The bewildering array of boxes for every purpose and in every style and design attests to the Victorian love of these practical table appointments. Every Silver and Silverplate manufacturer made them as music boxes and for jewelry gloves, cards, candy, cigars, tobacco, handkerchiefs, stamps, nick-nacks, trinkets, sewing items, pins, powder and cosmetics, etc.

They were made in all shapes and sizes with square or rectangular predominating. Designs ran the gamit from classic to rococo, in embossing, engraving, etc., and during the Art Nouveau period they were made with curvy undulating surfaces and typical floral and female nude motifs. Many of the Victorian boxes had cast novelty figural motifs and ingenious hinged drawers and swinging covers that could be opened by pushing a Cupid on a swing, a bird on a perch, etc. Cut glass inserts; Amberina, Ruby, Malachite, etc., in boxes andSilverplate mounts are most desirable and valuable, and the most difficult to find.

Values of particular pieces are entirely dependant upon working condition, size of box, decoration, etc.

Silverplate Boxes In Fine Working Condition
$30.00-$75.00

BOXES

Boxes in Fine Working Condition   Silverplate $30.00-$75.00

BOXES

Silverplate
$30.00-$75.00*

Sterling Silver
$50.00-$125.00*

*Price depends on size, design & condition

BOXES

Silverplate—$30.00-$75.00*
Silver—$50.00-$125.00*

Art Nouveau, c. 1909. Martele silver

*Depending On Size & Decoration

BOXES

TOBACCO & SNUFF BOXES

Sterling Silver—$20.00-$40.00
Silverplate—$15.00-$30.00

NOVELTY BOXES
Silverplate — $20.00-$55.00

BOXES

Silverplate
$40.00-$75.00
In Fine
Working
Condition

Silverplate—$30.00-$75.00

BRIDES' BASKETS

"Brides' Baskets" is a name applied to berry or fruit dishes made with an insert bowl of glass. Originally the Brides' Baskets were made of silver and silver gilt with pierced openwork, overall designs of flowers and with a carrying handle in the form of a silver ribbon bowknot. Fresh flowers could be placed in the basket. These Sterling silver fancies were made by Tiffany, Gorham, etc.

The Silverplate pieces were made by Meriden Brittania, Rogers & Bros., Wilcox Silver Co., and others with a frame standing on four low feet, a "basket handle" attached. Handles and stands were righly decorated in Rococo, Victorian and Classic motifs. The glass inserts were made in many patterns, from pressed etched, and cut clear or frosted glass. Much imported colored and Art Glass were used, including Amethyst, Agate, Amberina, Burmese, Cranberry, Peachblow, Pomona, Rubina Verde, Mary Gregory, etc. In the mid 1880's the ruffled, fluted irregular edge became popular. Complete original "Brides Baskets' of this period are difficult to find. The desirability of the art glass inserts resulted in collectors separating them from the Silverplated mounts. Imported reproductions are made and sold, reputable dealers would be the best source for original "Brides' Baskets."

BRIDES' BASKETS

With Clear Glass
$45.00—$65.00
With Cranberry Glass
$100.00—$200.00
With Pink Glass
$150.00—$200.00
With Satin Glass
$175.00—$300.00

For Original
Frames &
Glass In
Fine Condition

BRIDES' BASKETS

circa
1880

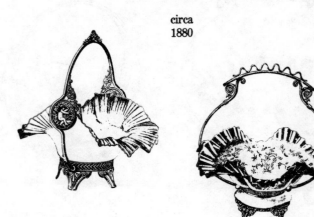

See previous page for prices

BRIDES' BASKETS

See Previous Page For Prices

BUTTER DISHES

To understand the need for these practical items, one must know that most butter was made at home on the farm. The extra butter produced on farms was sold to the closest market or store in one pound round cup-shaped molds, imprinted with "hallmark" of the housewife in the form of a butter "print."

Butter dishes of Britannia metal were made in the 1850's. By the 1880's butter dishes were produced by all silverplate manufacturers in a large variety of designs. Most were made with the same basic shape, a round truncated ball, the top half functioning as a cover that could be raised, or lifted and suspended from a hook in the arched handle, tilted back on hinges, or rolled under the base. The base platform was perforated to allow melted ice to drain. A clip containing a butter knife was often a part of the base. Elaborate birds, floral and baroque Victorian designs were engraved, embossed and chased on the base, legs, and cover. Cow finials were sometimes featured.

The double wall butter dish permitted the ice to be inserted in the space between the outside and inside wall of the dish.

Silverplate **$20.00-$85.00**
Silver **$100.00-$300.00**
Price Depends on Size, Design
Condition & Accessories

BUTTER DISHES

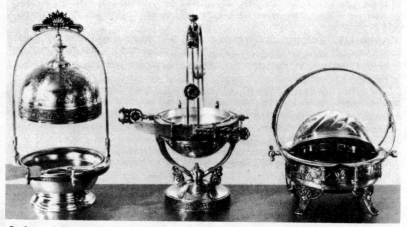

Left to right: Butter dish with hanging cover, made by Middletown Plate Co., c. 1885. Two butter dishes with revolving covers—shown open and partly closed—made by the Meriden Britannia Co. between 1882 and 1887.

See previous page for prices

Victorian, c. 1875

(cover open)

BREAD & CAKE BASKETS

These practical and attractive table items were introduced during the reign of George II and were made in Sterling Silver in a wide variety of designs and shapes.

About 1770, Sheffield plate baskets were introduced with the swing handle and decorated with piercing, chasing and engraving. They were oblong or oval in shape in imitation of the sterling silver models, and produced in large quantities, in hundreds of designs.

The silverplate baskets copied both the Sterling and Sheffield products. Ornamental handles and borders with grape and leaf, rope, beading, gadrooning, scrolling, and piercing were a feature of baskets of the 1860's. The bodies were engraved and chased in floral and baroque motifs. Classic medallions were often integrated with the overall designs.

By the 1870's and 1880's, cake baskets appeared on four foot, and often heavily decorated tall pedestals. The designs became typical of the period, over-embellished and very elaborate with molded cherubs, classic figures, birds, etc. Some baskets were "squared off" in the style of the 1870's. Surface decoration of these baskets were chased birds, cherubs, flowers, often inlaid with gold plate.

Silverplate
*$25.00-$125.00
Sterling
Silver
*$100.00-$300.00

Victorian, c. 1869
*Prices depend on design, size and weight of silver

104

CAKE BASKETS

VICTORIAN
circa 1870-1890

Silverplate
$25.00-$125.00
Silver
$100.00-$300.00

CANDELABRA

As a natural outgrowth of the single candlestick, the candelabra with its graceful arms was the decorative table lighting source of the 1700's and 1800's. In the latter half of the 1700's elaborate massive candelabras were made for the great houses of England and the Continent. Magnificent pieces with up to twelve lights were made for dining halls of wealth and aristocracy.

Sheffield plate, silver, and silverplate candelabras varied greatly in design and decoration reflecting the times, though the majority consisted of two branches with the center support having a removable finial and socket into which a third candle fitted. Candelabra with twisted and removable branches were a feature of Victorian dining tables enabling the multiple use of the individual elements; as seven, five, and three light units or individual candlesticks. Candelabra of typical Art Nouveau design used nudes, flowing hair ladies, floral forms, etc.

CHAMBERSTICKS & SNUFFERS

As the name implies these portable handled candle holders were made to light the way to the bed chamber of homes of the 1700's and 1800's. Early Silver and Silverplate models had a scissors type of snuffer, later the familiar "Dunce-Cap" conical snuffer was extensively used, and are more available to the collector.

CANDLESTICKS

The history of candle holders pre-dates Christian civilization.

As an important adjunct to Christian liturgy the candle holder reached a peak of artistic excellence during the period 500 A.D. to 1600, with elaborate designs in gold, silver, and precious stones. Many examples are on view in museums and churches. Cast simple candlesticks were made in large numbers in the early 1700's. These had gadrooned mouldings and were made of solid Sterling Silver. While styles in candlesticks were subject to the same influences as other Silver artifacts, the main thrust of design was Greek classic copied from the Ionic columns with fluted pillars and scrolled capitals.

Rococo motifs of the George II period introduced elaborate curlicues, swags, cartouches and floral embellishments. The classic and Rococo were the two primary design sources for Sheffield Plate and American candlesticks of the Victorian era. By the 1860's American Silverplate manufacturers were producing candlesticks in a large variety of sizes, shapes, and designs, including the typical Victorian use of cast figures such as mythological and literary characters, exotic birds and animals and fruits and flowers.

Handled candlesticks of this period were low socket candleholders on a drip disk, handles and bases were often heavily embellished.

The structure of Art Nouveau candlestick admirably combined the undulating female figure, long flowing hair, and floral and sea motifs. Again the Martele pieces individually created by the Gorham craftsmen are the most beautiful and valuable to be found. Candlesticks are sought and collected in pairs or sets of four.

CANDELABRA

PRICE RANGES

Silverplate	Silver
2 Arm—$15.00-$70.00 Each	2 Arm—$35.00-$100.00 Each
3 Arm—$20.00-100.00 Each	3 Arm—$50.00-$150.00 Each
4 Arm—$50.00-$200.00 Each	4 Arm—$75.00-$300.00 Each
5 Arm—$75.00-$350.00 Each	5 Arm—$200.00-$750.00 Each

All prices dependant upon size, design, silver weight and condition of the individual piece. Each quoted price is for a single piece. Matched pairs invariably bring in excess of twice the listed value.

CANDELABRA

See Previous Page For Prices

Art Nouveau candelabrum designed & patented by Albert Steffin, Assigned to the Pairpoint Corp. (Design Patent 36,875; April 12, 1904)

CANDELABRA

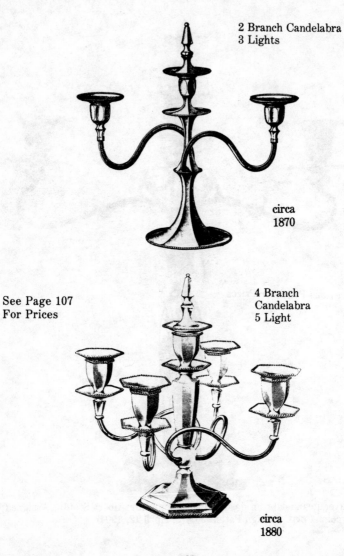

2 Branch Candelabra
3 Lights

circa
1870

See Page 107
For Prices

4 Branch
Candelabra
5 Light

circa
1880

CANDELABRA

ART NOUVEAU
circa 1904

See Page 107
For Prices

Silverplate
5 Branch
Candelabra

CANDELABRA

Art Nouveau — Martele Silver — circa 1906
6 Branch 7 Lights
See Page 107 for Prices

CANDELSTICKS

circa
1880

Silverplate
$35.00-$125.00 Pair*
Silver
$200.00-$600.00 Pair*

Chamber
Candlestick
Silverplate
$15.00-$50.00*
Silver
$35.00-$75.00*

*Depending on Height, Design, Weight of Silver.

CANDELSTICKS

ART
NOUVEAU
CANDLE
STICKS

**Silver
12″ high
$250.00**
circa 1900

MARTELÉ
GORHAM

CHAMBERSTICKS WITH SNUFFERS

Silverplate—$25.00-$100.00
Silver—$85.00-$225.00

ART NOUVEAU
MARTELE
circa 1902

CHAMBERSTICKS WITH SNUFFERS

MARTELÉ
GORHAM

ART NOUVEAU
circa 1902

See previous page for prices

CARD CASES

Card cases were carried by fashionable ladies of the Victorian era. American silver and silver plate makers produced them in a large variety of designs with floral or bird motifs engraved or embossed. Chains were attached so the cases could be carried. Plush or Morrocco boxes, into which the cases fit, were often sold with the cases.

Silverplate
$20.00-$50.00
Depending
On Decoration

Silver
$30.00-$95.00
Depending
On Decoration

CARD CASES

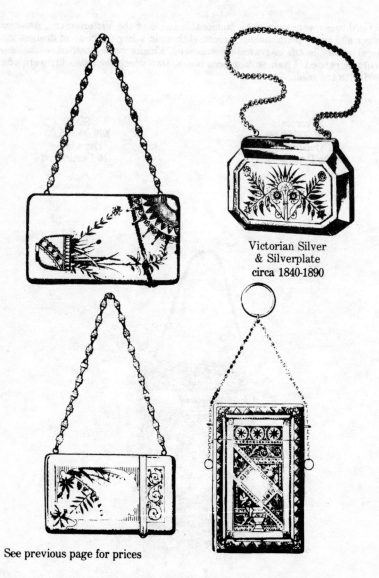

Victorian Silver
& Silverplate
circa 1840-1890

See previous page for prices

117

CARD TRAYS—CARD RECEIVERS

From the mid 1850's to World War I, card trays, or receivers, were made by every major silver plate manufacturer in an enormous variety of designs. The early ones were quite plain, but they evolved into etched, chased, embossed, hammered, and enameled trays, embellished with birds, animals, flowers, cherubs. Art glass vases set in holders were often combined with the trays.

Silverplate—**$40.00-$200.00**
Depending On Size & Decoration
Silverplate & Art Glass—**$90.00-325.00**
Depending on Glass, Size & Decoration

CARD RECEIVERS

Silverplate—circa 1865-1880

Silverplate & Art Glass   See Previous Page For Prices

CARD TRAYS & RECEIVERS

Silverplate
circa 1865-1880
$40.00-200.00
Silver
$90.00-$325.00

See Previous Page For Prices

CASTORS

Most tables of the Victorian era were graced with these decorative and practical receptacles for bottle containing spices and condiments. During the 1850's many varieties of the castor were patented including the "Ferris Wheel" type revolving castor.

The essential design of the castor was a Silverplate frame set on short legs or on a taller center pedestal. An ornate wide band circled the container that enclosed the bottles. Six bottles usually fitted in spaces provided. A pierced, or embossed handle rose in the center to be used to pass the castor at the table.

Designs ran riot on the castors of the late 1880's, a bewildering variety of frames and bottles were produced. Engraving, embossing and castings of every style and period were used—Rococo, Greek classic, Victorian and Oriental covered these dining table central pieces. Reed & Barton in the 1870's had a four bottle castor in a cart pulled by a proud peacock. Other manufacturers competed with their own elaborate creations. The 1880's tall revolving castors dominated in hundreds of varieties including four bottles, two bottle, and even one bottle.

Castor bottles were available in every range of glass decor, engraved, etched, cut, pressed, and in combinations of these techniques. Clear glass predominated, but blue, ruby, amber, and green were made in cut glass designs.

Breakfast castors often had egg cups and egg spoons and were limited to three or four bottles.

Castor handles could be purchased separately and were offered with call bells or vases included. Bottles also were a separate item featured in catalogs of the times.

Because of the value and desirability of Castor bottles to Art glass collectors, many became separated from the original frames. Now, with the value of Victorian Silverplate items increasing, complete castor sets with good intact cut or engraved bottles, especially those in color complete with tops, are bringing top prices.

Salt & Pepper Castor
(opalescent glass, found
in assorted colors)
Silverplate—$35.00-$75.00

CASTORS

Castors
Silverplate
$50.00-$225.00*
Silver
$100.00-$350.00*

Handsome 6 bottle dinner castor with deer head ornaments. Product of the Meriden Britannia Co. and made between 1885 and 1867. Height 18 inches.

*Price Depends On Number & Type of Bottles, Conditon.

CASTORS

Silverplate
$50.00-$225.00
Silver
$100.00-$350.00

ALL
circa
1880

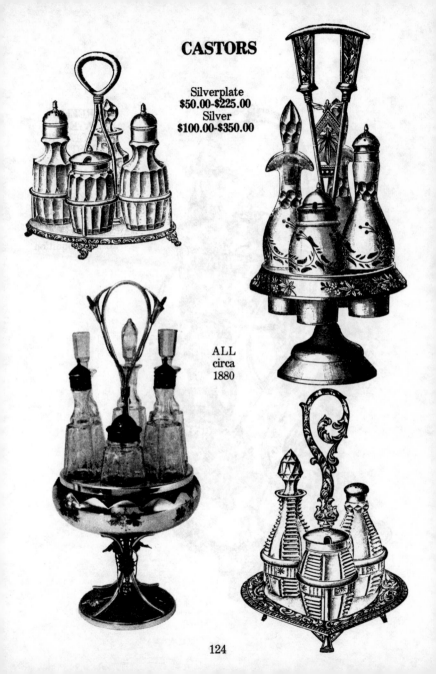

CASTORS

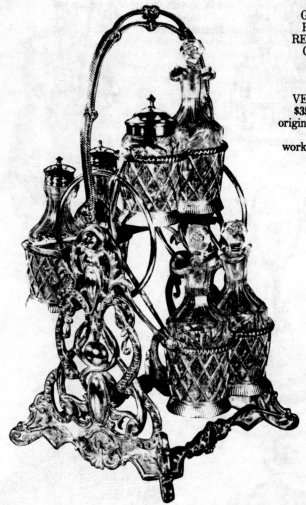

GREEN'S
PATENT
REVOLVING
CASTOR
circa
1860

VERY RARE
$350.00 with
original bottles and
in good
working condition

125

CASTORS—PICKLE CASTORS

Closely related to Dinner & Breakfast Castors is this decorative and practical novelty item of 1870-1900.

The Pickle Castor consisted of a Silverplate frame with handle, tongs, or fork, and a round glass insert with a knob-top Silverplate cover.

Elaborate and fancy designs in pickle castors proliferated. Frames, handles, and tongs were coordinated with the same design theme repeated on all pieces.

The glass inserts were made of pressed, cut or engraved, or decorated glass. Most bottles were clear glass, but cut-glass in amber, blue, green and cranberry were available. Cut and molded glass bottles of Rubina Verde, Satin Glass, Amberina, Peachblow, Agata, etc. were made, and offered in catalogs of the 1880's as selections to be combined with castor frames.

Complete original castors with Cut Glass or Art Glass bottles are rare and quite valuable.

All Made of Silverplate
Clear Or Pressed Glass: $50.00-$80.00
Art Glass; Amber, Blue, Red: $85.00-$250.00
Price Depends On Design & Glass Bottle

circa
1870

CASTORS—PICKLE CASTORS

Clear Glass—$50.00-$80.00
Art Glass—$85.00-$250.00

CELERY STANDS

Between 1860 and 1900 these practical table items were very popular for serving celery stalks. The tall silverplate stands were made with a large variety of glass during the 1800's—glass inserts were: pressed, cut crystal, engraved, clear, frosted, and colored glass of all types: Ruby, Amberina, Cranberry, Peachblow, Venetian Thread, Burmese, etc.

The two types of celery holders are, the tall stand on a pedestal, and low rectangular cut glass trays set in footed Silverplate frames. The frames were elaborately decorated in design motifs of the Victorian period.

Silverplate
$30.00-$100.00

Price Depends
On Glass.
Art Glass
Most Valuable

VICTORIAN
circa 1870-1895

CENTERPIECES—MANTEL ORNAMENTS

A great variety of these cast figures were produced in the 1880's and 1890's. They ranged in size from a few inches to two feet in height. The subjects ranged over many areas representing mythological and classic figures: Appolo, Mars, Dying Gladiator, Arabs, Indian Chief, Indian Squaw, etc., animals of all types, domestic and wild; dogs, deer, wolves, buffalo, lions, bears, etc.

These cast figures were usually made of so-called "White Metal," and silver plated, or gold or gilt plated. Some were made of Sterling Silver, such as the Gorham Mfg. Co. Martele centerpiece with nymph figure handles and Art Nouveau floral decorations.

Though these ornaments were made for centerpiece decorative purposes, many of these same figures appeared on mantel clocks of the period. They were also adapted to use as lamp bases and these pieces are found with holes drilled.

Silverplate—$20.00-$100.00
Depending on Size & Subject
American Indians Are Most Valuable

Silver—$100.00-$300.00
Depending on Size & Silverweight

GORHAM   ART
MARTELÉ   NORVEAU
                circa 1895

CENTERPIECES

Silverplate
$20.00-$100.00
Silver
$100.00-$300.00

CENTERPIECES—MANTLEPIECES

See previous page for prices

CENTERPIECES—MANTLEPIECES

Silverplate $20.00-$100.00
Silver $100.00-$300.00

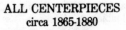

ALL CENTERPIECES
circa 1865-1880

American Indian Subjects
Are Most Valuable

CHAFING DISHES

The chafing dish was known in Old England in the 1500's. Throughout the centuries it evolved to the form it is known today, an inner container for the food, the outer container filled with hot water heated by a burner.

The chafing dishes of the late 1800's were made by many American silverplate manufacturers. They used alcohol burners and stood on either three or four legs. They were made both with and without handles, and were often elaborately decorated in the Victorian or Art Nouveau style. These chafing dishes were heated by alcohol burners. Complete units with stands and burners are the most valuable.

Silverplate $100.00-$350.00
Sterling Silver $200.00-$600.00

Depends upon size, design, condition

Chafing Dish

133

CHILDREN'S SILVER & SILVERPLATE

Small porringers and "Pap Boats" and "Pap Spoons" were child feeding implements used in the 1700's. These were made by American silversmiths and often had engraved simple designs.

By the 1850's the popularity of silver children's items as gifts for children and their parents resulted in a proliferation of many products. These included: Bowls, porringers, pap boats, pap spoons, cup sets, christening sets, whistles, rattles, napkin rings, spoons, etc.

Nursery rhymes were the source of much of the design and embellishments used on these pieces. Etching, engraving, chasing, repousse, and embossing were the techniques used to decorate children's items. Animals of all types, especially dogs and cats, were also a popular motif.

During the 1930's Mickey Mouse, Donald Duck, and other cartoon characters were used as subjects on silver children's spoons, forks, and sets. These are sought after by collectors of Disney and comic characters.

The Gorham Silver Company produced many children's items. The most expensive and unique were the Martele pieces; plates, mugs, porringers, etc., individually made by Gorham silversmiths.

Children's silverware items are a good area of endeavor for the new collector.

Silverplate
Rattles & Whistle, etc.—**$18.00-$40.00**
Baby Brush, Combs, etc.—**$20.00-$50.00**
Cups, Spoons, Porringers—**$15.00-$35.00**

Sterling Silver
Rattles, Rattle & Whistle, Etc.—**$30.00-$85.00***
Baby Brush, Combs, etc.—**$40.00-$100.00**
Cups, Spoons, Porringers—**$30.00-$85.00**

Price Depends On Design, Size, Condition
*If Made with ivory, Mother of Pearl, etc.

CHILDREN'S SILVER WHISTLES & RATTLES

For prices see page 134

CHILDREN'S SILVER ITEMS

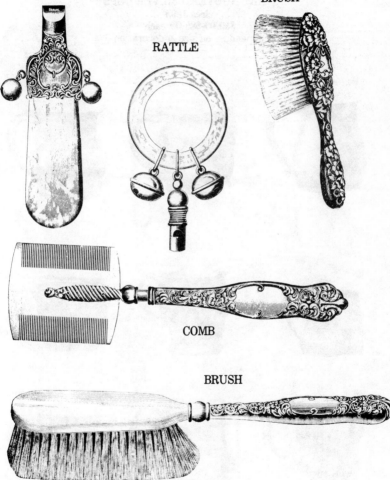

WHISTLE & RATTLE

RATTLE

BRUSH

COMB

BRUSH

See page 134 for prices

CHILDREN'S SILVER CUPS

ART NOUVEAU SILVER CUPS
circa 1895
$30.00-$85.00 each
depending on size & decoration

CHILDREN'S CUPS

Silverplate $15.00-$35.00
Silver $40.00-$90.00

circa
1870-1890

CHILDREN'S CUPS

Silverplate $15.00-$35.00
Silver $40.00-$90.00

Note: Cups With Matching Spoons
Are Rare & Valuable

COFFEE POTS & URNS

While not as popular and widely used as tea pots, many fine examples of silver coffee pots were made in England and Europe from late 1600's to the 1800's. In general the design and shape emulated tea pots of similar times.

American silver and silverplate producers made coffee pots as a part of tea sets and advertised by them as such. The coffee pot was usually very similar in shape and design to the tea pot but was taller.

After dinner coffee pots became a popular individual table item in the late 1880's. They were made in long necked exotic shapes in the fashion of Turkish, Moorish, Persian, and East Indian originals.

After dinner, or black coffee sets, in these motifs were made by Gorham, Wm. Kirk & Son, Reed & Barton, Tiffany & Company and others. The Sterling Silver sets of this period are increasing rapidly in value.

COFFEE POTS
Silverplate
$50.00-$175.00
Silver
$75.00-$250.00

CIRCA 1861

COFFEE POTS

GORHAM—VICTORIAN circa 1890

SILVERPLATE—$50.00-$175.00
Silver $75.00-$225.00

COFFEE POTS & URNS

Silverplate
$80.00-$200.00
Silver
$400.00-$900.00

circa 1878

CREAMERS (MILK JUGS)

The addition of hot milk to tea served in England in early 1700 required an appropriate Silver serving vessel. Hot milk jugs were practical table items with handle and spout on a variety of body shapes: helmet, oval, baluster, octagonal, etc. Many early designs were simple and classic but by the mid 1700's, more elaborate embellishments such as casting and chasing, piercing and scroll-work featuring animal and classic figures appeared. The creamer stood on a single pedestal, three ball feet, or flat on its base, they are known both with and without hinged cover.

By the Victorian period the creamer had been relegated to an adjunct to the serving of tea or coffee and its design was complimentary to the rest of the set. Beading and engraving and applied medallions were popular decorative motifs.

Individual creamers are not nearly as desirable or valuable as complete sugar and cream sets.

Silverplate $15.00-$35.00
Sterling Silver $50.00-$175.00

Sugar & Creamer Sets
Silverplate $20.00-80.00
Sterling Silver $90.00-$215.00

Prices Depend On Design, Size, Condition & Weight of Silver.

DESK SETS—INKSTANDS

The Inkstand had its beginnings in Colonial America. Sterling silver canoe-shaped inkstands, holding cut glass ink bottles on low legs of the 1790's were superseded by oblong trays of the early 1800's with gadrooned rims, holding cut glass bottles. The Victorian inkstand and Desk sets featured rococo piercing, casting and engraving of the most elaborate type, sitting on low floral feet, and made in fanciful designs with animal figures, birds, and classic human figures. Inkstands in combinations of pottery and silver, wood and silver, and glass and silver deposit were made.

The Victorian Inkstands, or Inkwells, held one or two glass bottles with Sterling Silver or Silverplated hinged tops. Desk sets with open trays, or holders, calendars, stamp boxes, pen wipers, and blotters, were produced in a large variety of designs. Art Nouveau Inkstands in Sterling Silver were produced in various floral and sea-motif, mermaids, exotic fish, sea-wave, nude figures, cherubs, flowing haired ladies, etc., by Gorham in Martele silver. These Inkstands, some with candle holders, are among the most beautiful and valuable ever created. The Unger Brothers of Newark also produced unusual Sterling Silver Art Nouveau Inkstands.

Silverplate & Crystal
2 Bottles & Tray

$30.00-$70.00

Silver
$50.00-$150.00

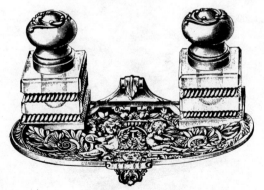

Inkstand, circa 1870

DESK SETS—INKSTANDS

Desk Set, $200.00-$250.00

Inkstand, circa 1870
Silverplate and crystal $50.00-$80.00

DESK SETS—INKSTANDS

Martelle Silver & Crystal—$250.00-$300.00
Art Nouveau—circa 1885

Martele Silver Inkstand with Candleholder
Art Nouveau, circa 1895
$200.00-$300.00

146

DESK SETS—INKSTANDS

All Prices
Quoted Are For
Silverplate

Silver Prices
Double

Saturday
December
24

$35.00-$50.00

Thursday
March
11th.

$50.00-$80.00

$65.00-$90.00

147

INDIVIDUAL INK BOTTLES AND INKWELLS

A large selection of individual ink bottles in cut, pressed, and etched glass, with Silver and Silverplate hinged tops were produced in the 1880's - 1920's. The tops are in Victorian, Rococo, or Art Nouveau designs. Many can still be found in Antique shops at reasonable prices.

Sterling Silver Inkwells with glass inserts and no tops in Art Nouveau cylinders were made by most manufacturers. Unger Brothers of Newark produced fine examples of this item in various designs.

Silverplate & Crystal
Single Bottle & Stand
$20.00-$75.00
Price Depends on Design
Silver & Crystal
$35.00-$140.00

Martele Silver and Crystal Ink Bottle and Tray
Art Nouveau circa 1895
$175.00-$225.00

INDIVIDUAL INK BOTTLES & INKWELLS

Martele
Silver &
Crystal
Inkbottle
Art Nouveau
circa 1895
$75.00-$135.00

Inkstand

See page 148 for prices

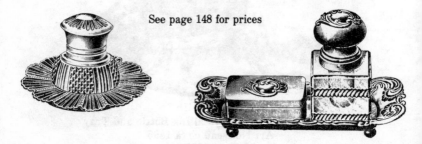

See Page 148 For Prices

OTHER DESK FURNISHINGS

These include stamp boxes, paper knives, letter openers, calenders, erasers, pen holders, letter clips, pen trays, racks, blotters, pen wipers, seals, book marks, paper shears, glue pots, etc. were all subject to the attention of the Victorian and Art Nouveau designers of Silver and Silverplate. Embossing, engraving, chasing covered all exposed surfaces. Stamp boxes are sometimes mistaken for hairpin boxes. To distinguish between them: The stamp box has a rounded bottom, the hairpin box is flat.

Prices This Page
Silverplate—$15.00-$40.00
Silver—$30.00-$75.00
Price Depends On Design

Blotter

Stamp Box

Thermometer

Letter File

Stamp and Pen Tray

DESK FURNISHINGS
PAPER KNIVES

Silver
Handle
$30.00-$55.00

Silver
Art
Nouveau
1904
$60.00-$100.00

Sterling,
Martele
$30.00-$50.00
Each

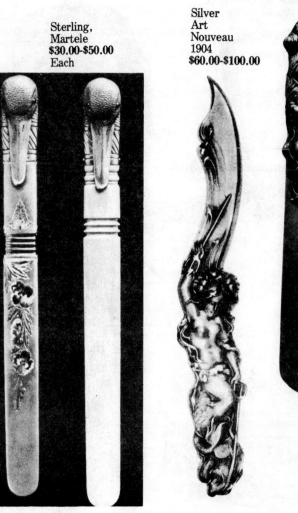

DESK FURNISHINGS

THERMOMETERS, CALENDARS, BLOTTERS

Silverplate—$10.00-$50.00
Silver—$20.00-$90.00

Calendar

Stationery Holder and Calendar

Blotter and Calendar Combined.

Daily Calendar

Thermometer

DESK FURNISHINGS
SILVER BOOK MARKS

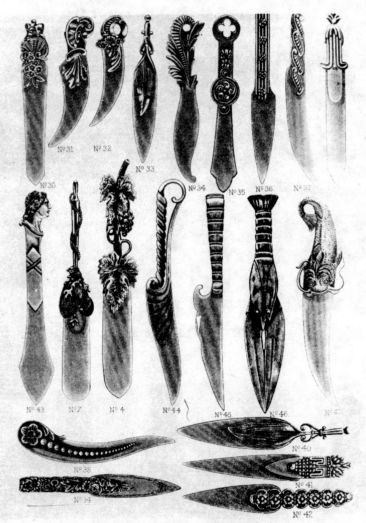

No 31 No 32
No 33
No 30 No 34 No 35 No 36 No 37

No 43 No 7 No 4 No 44 No 45 No 46 No 47

No 38
No 40
No 41
No 14 No 42

Silver Book Marks—$15.00-$35.00

DESK FURNISHINGS
CUT GLASS INKWELLS—SILVER TOPS

Silver Tops & Cut Crystal Bottles—**$20.00-$75.00***

LETTER CLIPS—SILVER

$20.00-$45.00

*Price Depends on Size of Bottle

DESK FURNISHINGS
SILVER PENS, ERASERS

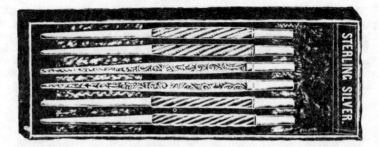

pen holders

Silver Penholders
$20.00-$35.00

Prices depend
upon design

erasers
$10.00-$15.00

FERN DISHES & FLOWER POTS

The Victorian love of flowers and green plants manifested itself in these silver-plated fern dishes and flower pots, that held linings of porcelain, pottery, and metal. Most fern dishes were round in shape but oblong shapes are known. They often had handles attached to the outside casings and sat on low feet. Designs were Victorian Rococo frequently in open fretwork. Flower pots were similar in form and design to Fern Dishes though they were taller and usually had a flat base.

Silverplate—**$30.00-$80.00**
Depending on Size & Decorations

Silver—**$60.00-$200.00**
Price depends on size, weight of
silver & decorations

Fern Dish, circa 1870

FERN DISHES & FLOWER POTS
CIRCA 1870-1900

Fern Dish

Flower Pot

Fern Dish

See previous page for prices

Fern Dish

FERN DISHES & FLOWER POTS

circa 1870-1900

Silverplate
$30.00-$80.00
Silver
$60.00-$200.00
Price depends
on size &
weight &
design

Flower Pot

Fern Dish

Fern Dish

FORKS

Forks as we know them today orignated in Italy during the early 1500's perhaps as a by-product of the Renaissance and the resurgence of cleanliness and manners of the period.

The fork was introduced to England in the 1600's as an eating utensil, prior to this forks were used only as serving pieces.

Until the early 1700's travelling forks were the rule and were carried along with a table knife by those who travelled.

In pre-Civil War America, simple table forks made of coin silver were used. These usually had four prongs and the typical "Fiddle Back" of the times. Like the coin silver spoons, the initials of the owner were often engraved on the handle, and the maker's mark was stamped on the underside of the stem.

American forks of the Victorian and Post-Civil War period (1865-1900) proliferated in a very large variety of designs and types. Featured in catalogs of silver manufacturers of the times were such items as; Fish Forks, Lettuce Forks, Ice Cream Forks, Tomato Forks, Cucumber Forks, Cold Meat Forks, Sardine Forks, Oyster and Pickle Forks, Berry Forks, Salad Forks, etc.

Like the spoons of Victorian times the design and embellishments on serving and dining forks were in every style and fashion.

Classic, Rococo, Romanesque, Floral, Art Nouveau designs appeared on handle, stems, and prongs. Prongs ranged from two prong berry forks, to six prong fish forks. Prongs were straight curved, or arrow shaped.

Individual large serving forks are rising in value and still may be found in antique stores and flea markets.

Sets of 4, 6, 8, 12, 14, etc. in the same pattern are valuable particularly in sterling silver. Since most patterns were made in both sterling and silverplate, knowledge of the makers' marks is important.

FORKS

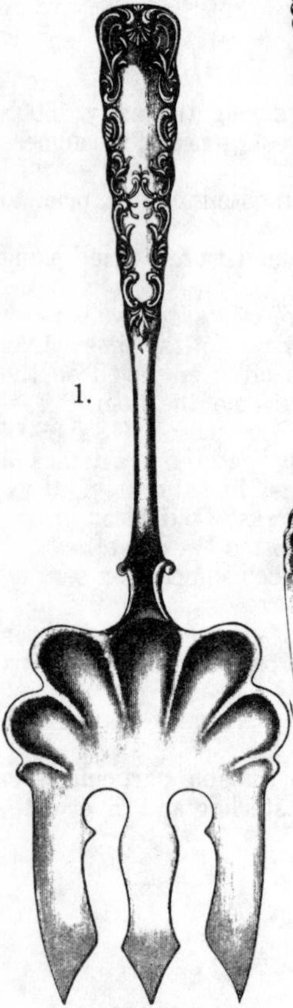

Fish Fork

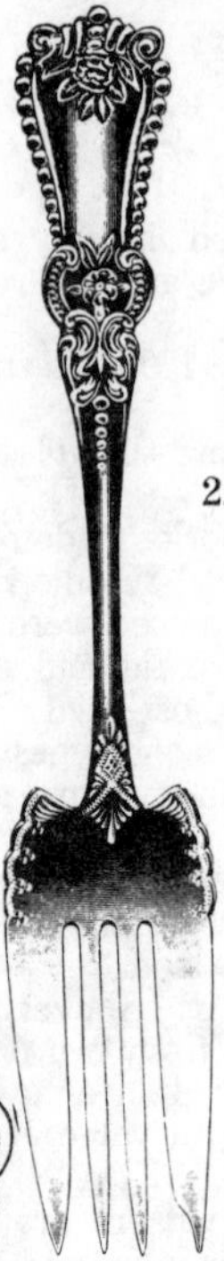

Cold Meat, Cake & Salad Forks

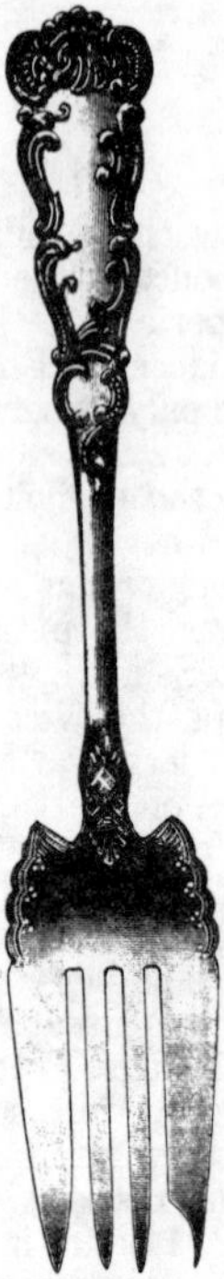

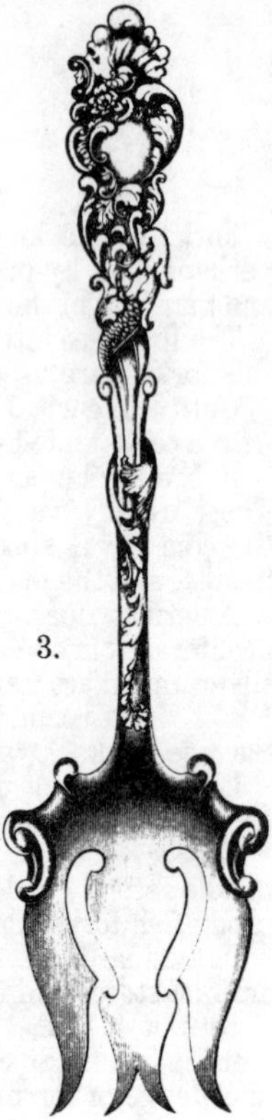

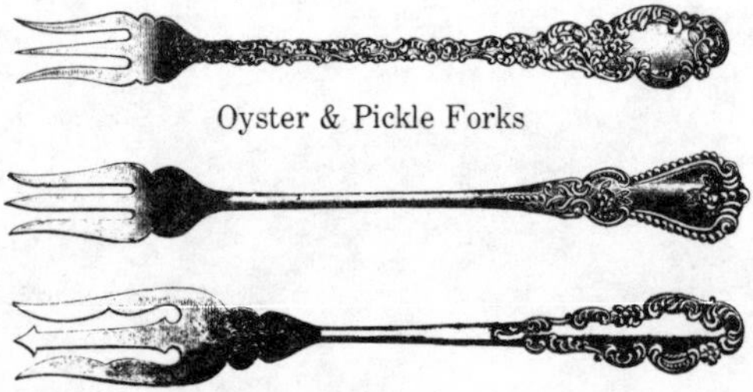

Oyster & Pickle Forks

Silver
1. $75.00-$125.00
2. $30.00-$70.00
3. $40.00-$80.00
4. $9.50-$30.00

NOTE: Silverplate Prices are about 1/2 quoted prices.

FORKS

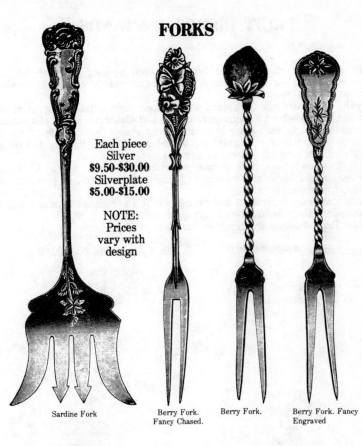

Each piece
Silver
$9.50-$30.00
Silverplate
$5.00-$15.00

NOTE:
Prices
vary with
design

Sardine Fork

Berry Fork.
Fancy Chased.

Berry Fork.

Berry Fork. Fancy
Engraved

ART NOUVEAU

Silver Bread Fork
$100.00-$200.00

FRUIT DISHES & STANDS

The early fruit stands of the 1860's featured pressed glass, or cut and engraved crystal on silver plated frames, and stands of simple beaded, gadrooned, or engraved designs.

By the mid 1870's, the fruit stand was the focal point of the dining table. The base and the glass bowl became more ornate and elaborate. Silver plate manufacturers vied with each other in creating fruit stands featuring floral motifs, cherubs, birds, fantastic animals, classic and mythological figures, and rococo motifs on either a center pedestal or four low feet.

The glass bowls were made in many varieties of art glass: Agata, Amberina, Burmese, Satin, Malachite, Peachblow, clear, colored, etc., in pressed, cut, engraved, or etched form.

Fruit stands are difficult to find complete with their glass containers, due to breakage and their desireability to art glass collectors.

Note: Reproductions are imported from foreign countries.

Silver—**$100.00-$300.00**   Silverplate—**$100.00-$200.00**

"Tree of Life"
Pattern Bowl
circa 1880

Cut
Crystal
Bowl
circa
1875

FRUIT DISHES & STANDS

Price depends upon design,
type of glass insert.
Cut Crystal & Art Glass
are the most valuable

FRUIT DISH
circa 1880

All illustrated on
this page are
of silverplate

See Previous Page For Prices

GENTLEMEN'S ACCESSORIES

Although ladies vanity and toilet accessories were the greatest subject of Silver and Silverplate products, the gentlemen of 1860—1915 were not neglected. Shaving items such as: shaving mugs, cups, and brushes (fixed and folding), soap boxes, silver and silverplate mounted razor strops, razors with Silver and Silverplate handles were available. Shoe horns and whisk brooms and collar-button boxes, pocket knives, and pocket flasks, canes, and umbrella heads, watches and watch fobs all were designed and embellished in the height of Victorian and Art Nouveau fashion.

SHAVING BRUSHES

The brush handles of Silver and Silverplate were heavily embossed, engraved, and chased in a large variety of designs, Victorian, Rococo, and Art Nouveau. Folding brushes enabled the bristles to recess into the hollow handles for travelling. Due to deteriation brushes complete with original bristles are hard to find.

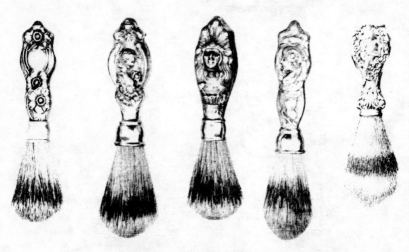

Silverplate $10.00-$30.00
Silver

GENTLEMEN'S ACCESSORIES

SHAVING MUGS AND CUPS AND SETS

Single-handled cups and mugs were used along with shaving soap and brushes to create lather for shaving. Handles and bodies were highly decorated, and the owner's name often engraved. Matching mugs and brushes in Sterling Silver were made from 1880-1915 and are most sought-after and valuable. Complete shaving sets wiht tilting mirror mug, and stand containing a drawer for razor are also rare and valuable in complete, original condition.

Shaving Mug and Brush

Depending upon design and condition, prices range from **$50.00** to **$100.00** in silverplate and from **$80.00** to **$125.00** in sterling.

GENTLEMEN'S ACCESSORIES
SHAVING MUGS & CUPS & SETS

SHAVING SET
WITH DRAWER FOR RAZOR
Silverplate—$125.00-$160.00

GENTLEMEN'S ACCESSORIES

RAZORS

The gentleman's shaving razor of Victorian times (1840-1900) was an object of much embellishment. Sterling Silver, Sheffield plate, and Silverplate were combined with ivory, horn, tortoiseshell, mother of pearl, etc., and embossed, engraved and inlaid into an enormous variety of designs. Art Nouveau razors reflected the flowing and floral designs of the period.

Silverplate
$20.00-$40.00
Silver
$75.00-$200.00

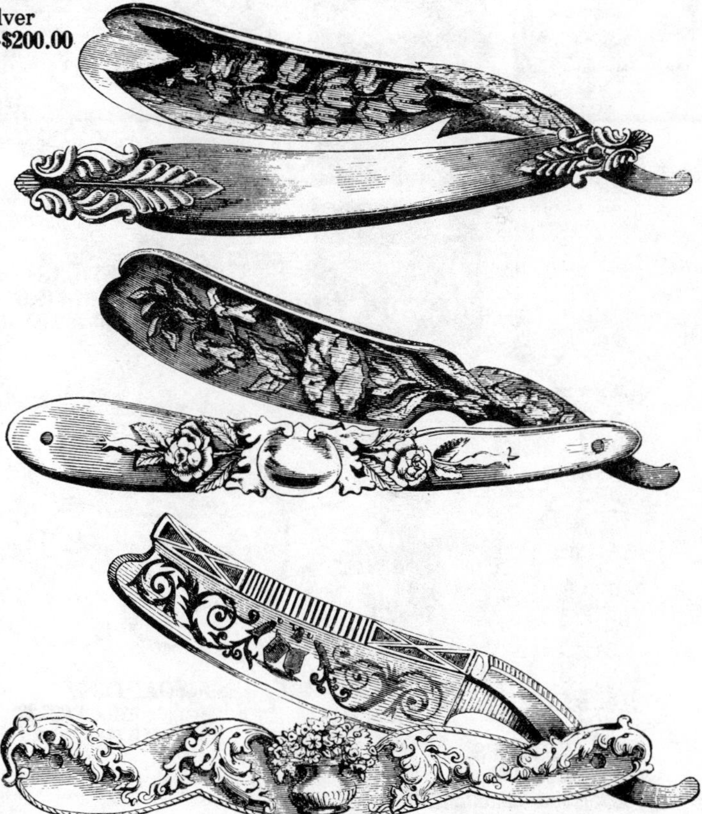

GENTLEMEN'S ACCESSORIES

SOAP BOXES, SHAVE STICKS AND RAZOR STROPS

Silver and Silverplate accessories connected with shaving were numerous. Round and square covered boxes for holding shave soap, shave stick boxes, tube shaped with covers for travelling, all decorated in the Victorian and Art Nouveau fashion.

Leather razor strops were made in Silver and Silverplated mountings with designs typical of Victorian and Rococo influence.

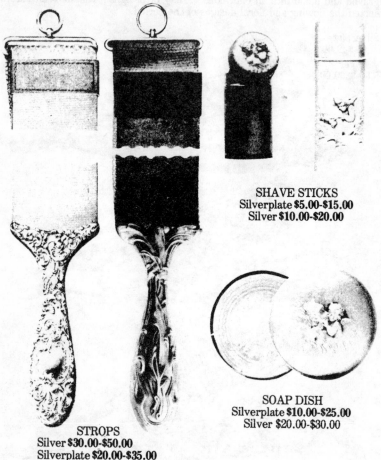

SHAVE STICKS
Silverplate $5.00-$15.00
Silver $10.00-$20.00

SOAP DISH
Silverplate $10.00-$25.00
Silver $20.00-$30.00

STROPS
Silver $30.00-$50.00
Silverplate $20.00-$35.00

GENTLEMEN'S ACCESSORIES

CANES, WALKING STICKS, UMBRELLA HANDLES (HEADS)

By the late 1800's most American gentlemen carried silver or gilt-headed canes. Many Silver and Silverplate firms made these masculine status symbols and it was not uncommon for the Victorian man to own several. The "mushroom cap" engraved, etched, and embossed with scrolls and strapwork and top space for a monogram was the most popular type.

These were made in straight cap, round cap, octagon cap, etc. Also popular were the "L" shaped square crook, curve crook, polo crook and the "C" shaped fancy crook.

Canes with heads of silver deposit, combined with Ivory staghorn, and other materials are rare and quite valuable.

These same cane and walking stick handles (crooks) were used on umbrellas as well.

Square Crook.

Sterling
Silver
Crooks—**$35.00-$60.00**
Heads—**$20.00-$40.00**
Complete Canes
With Crooks or
Heads—**Double Price**

Curve Crook.

GENTLEMEN'S ACCESSORIES
CANES, WALKING STICKS, UMBRELLA HANDLES (HEADS)

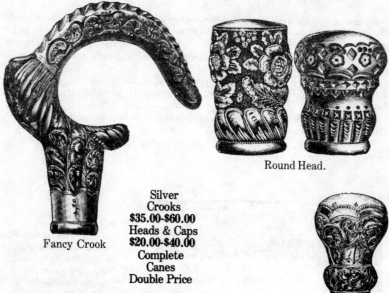

Fancy Crook

Silver
Crooks
$35.00-$60.00
Heads & Caps
$20.00-$40.00
Complete
Canes
Double Price

Round Head.

Round Head.

Square Round Crooks.

Round Cap.

GENTLEMEN'S ACCESSORIES

POCKET FLASKS

Silver and Silverplated pocket flasks were among the articles made for gentlemen from the 1800's through the 1920's. In general they were simple oval shapes "pumpkin seed" with screw-top closings. Prohibition "hip-flasks" were curved to fit the back pocket.

They were often made of mementoes to commemorate a patriotic or festive occasion with embossed or engraved designs illustrating the event.

The Art Nouveau period (1895-1910) produced many examples with typical designs of sinuous females embossed on the flasks.

Silver
& Cut Crystal
$50.00-$90.00
Prices depend
on size of flask
& design of
glass bottle insert.

Silver
$35.00-$75.00

Silverplate
$20.00-$50.00

GENTLEMEN'S ACCESSORIES

DRESS ITEMS

Sterling Silver and silverplate shoe horns, button hooks, whisk brooms and collar-button boxes were an important part of the Victorian man's personal and dress accoutrements. The prevailing whimsy of the period showed in a collar button box in the round shape of an embossed collar and bow with the word "collar" engraved and a button as the cover handle.

A silverplate whisk broom with a liquor flask in the handle has the legend "JUST A FEW" and three birds in flight (swallows) engraved on the body.

Cuff links in all styles and designs in Sterling and Silverplate were worn in the late 1800's. Many examples are to be found today in antique shops and flea markets.

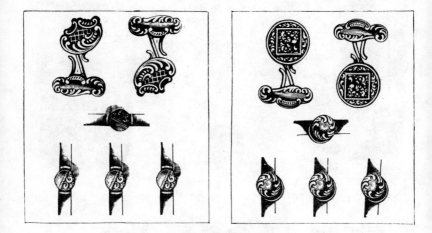

Button Boxes
Silverplate
$10.00-$20.00
Silver
$17.00-$35.00

Button Box

Cuff Links
Silver **$10.00-$15.00**

Sets of
Links, Studs & Tack
Silver **$20.00-$50.00**

GENTLEMEN'S ACCESSORIES

DRESS ITEMS

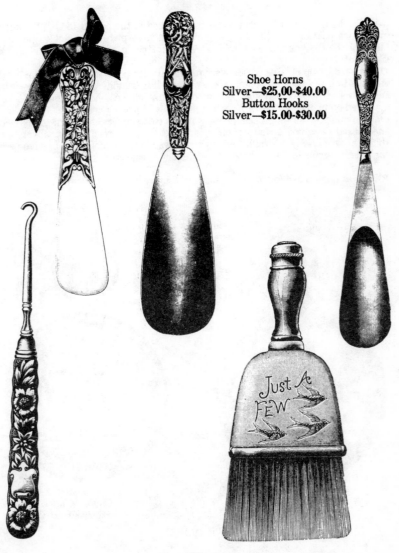

Shoe Horns
Silver—$25,00-$40.00
Button Hooks
Silver—$15.00-$30.00

Just A
Few

GENTLEMEN'S ACCESSORIES

POCKET WATCHES

While the majority of pocket watches produced in the period 1865-1910, were made with gold or gold-filled cases, silver and silverplate were not neglected. Many of the designs made in gold were duplicated in either sterling silver or silverplate.

A special group of silver cases were produced with popular themes etched and engraved on the backs of open-face watches. Illustrations of typical American subjects such as: locomotives, steamboats, fire engines, horses, indians, etc. appeared on many watches. Inlays of gold and gold plating created a "two-color" effct on many of these. Hunting case watches (with covers) featuring embossed and chased designs are rising rapidly in value. Those with matching silver link chains are especially desirable. As with gold watches, chronographs in silver are the most valuable in the pocket watch category of collectibles.

All prices quoted are for original pieces in fine working condition.

Silver Cases
Plain—$25.00-$75.00
Silver Cases
Engraved Backs
$65.00-$200.00

"Locomotive"

"Horseman"

GENTLEMEN'S ACCESSORIES
POCKET WATCHES

Silver, Open Face
Chronograph

"Steamboat"

Silver Cases
Plain $25.00-$75.00

Silver Cases
Engraved Backs
$65.00-$200.00

All Prices
For Watches
In Fine
Working
Condition

"King of the Forest"

"Fire Engine"

GENTLEMEN'S ACCESSORIES
SILVER VEST CHAINS

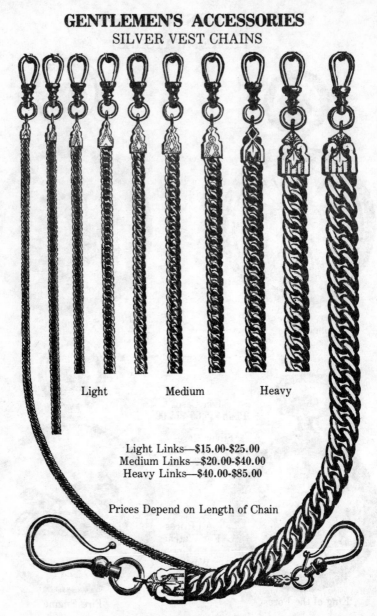

Light   Medium   Heavy

Light Links—$15.00-$25.00
Medium Links—$20.00-$40.00
Heavy Links—$40.00-$85.00

Prices Depend on Length of Chain

KNIVES
TABLE AND CARVING KNIVES

The history of knives antedates that of forks, though knives with silver handles were not made before 1700. In earlier times in England, men carried a sheathed knife that was used both for defense and for eating. The introduction of silver handled table knives in the beginning of the eighteenth century ended the use of sheath knife at the dining table.

Many handle designs, pistol handle shape, reeded forms, plain forms, the shell motif, etc., originating in this period were later copied in the Victorian era, 1840 - 1900. Carving knives, and carving sets, bread knives and sets, were produced by all American silver and silverplate manufacturers in a variety of styles and types. Many had stag horn handles with silver pommels. Blades generally were of steel on these knives and when a silver or silverplate handle was used, the embellishment was rococo or floral in the Victorian fashion.

Desert knives, table knives, fruit knives, butter knives, etc., were made in the table-setting patterns of each manufacturer, the handles reflecting the rococo, Victorian, and Art Nouveau influences in etched, or embossed designs. Mother-of-Pearl or ivory were often combined with silver on the handles.

Matching sets of 4,6,8,12,14,24, etc., are collectable, valuable, and saleable. Individual place-setting knives are of less value.

FISH KNIFE
*Silver†
$45.00-$125.00

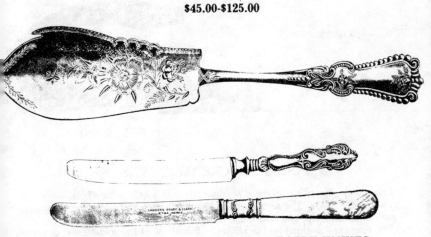

TABLE KNIVES
Silver†
$8.50-$15.00

*Price Depends on Design, Pattern, Weight.
†Note: Silverplate ½-Quoted Prices.

178

KNIVES
CARVING KNIVES AND SETS

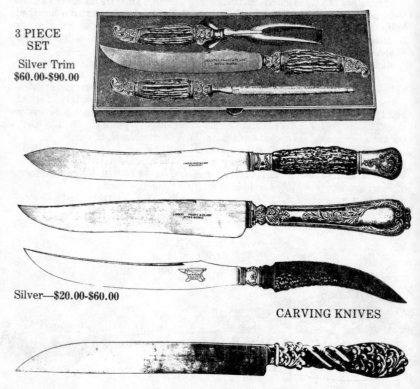

3 PIECE
SET

Silver Trim
$60.00-$90.00

Silver—$20.00-$60.00

CARVING KNIVES

BREAD KNIFE

FISH & ICE CREAM KNIVES

Triangular shaped and pierced sterling silver fish knives, or slices, were used in the middle 1700's. The asymmetrical shape fish slice had a single cutting edge, a curved pointed tip, and was made completely of silver.

The engraved designs on the blades of fish slices of the mid-1800's, generally had a fish motif as the subject. During the Victorian period the popular foliate scrolls and floral motifs appeared on the blades and handles. Ice cream knives, or slicers, were similar to fish slices, though smaller in size and less elaborately engraved.

KNIVES

JACK KNIVES—POCKET KNIVES

These charming, folding pocket knives were made by all silver and silverplate manufacturers: Rogers Bros., Gorham, Samuel Kirk, Unger Bros., etc., from 1860-1920.

They were advertised as "Fruit Knives" and usually had one curved blade with a single cutting edge. Often a "Nut Pick" blade accompanied the cutting blade. The "Nut Pick" was a slender curved bar used to extract the meat from the nut. Victorian designs were embossed, etched, or engraved on the body and handle of the pocket knife. Mother-of-Pearl, ivory, ebony, etc. were inlaid on sterling or silverplate on some models. Fruit Knives are growing rapidly in value and interest to collectors.

Silverplate—$7.50-$35.00
Silver—$10.00-$50.00
Price Depends on Size, Design,
Inlays, Ivory, Pearl Etc.

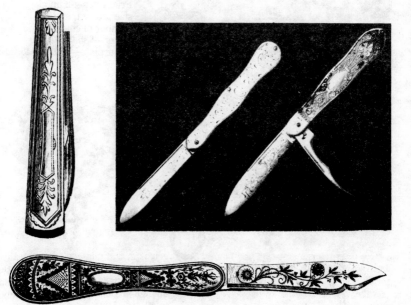

LADIES' ITEMS

CHATELAINES

The American Silversmiths turned their attention to the production of practical and decorative items for ladies of the Victorian and Art Nouveau eras. Purses, pins of all types, pin holders, chatelaines, buckles, clasps, veil holders, combs, glove hooks, opera glasses, Vinaigrettes and glove colognes, etc.

Design motifs used on these feminine pieces ranged from Victorian rococo thru Art Nouveau with the emphasis on flowery forms, cherubs and nymphs, ladies heads with flowing tresses and birds of every type at rest and in flight. Many of these feminine artifacts are to be found in quantity antique shops, flea markets and other sources.

CHATELAINES

Dating back to earliest history the chatelaine was a decorative and practical small flat plate with a flat hook that fitted into the waistband and had three or more chains suspended, holding a watch, smelling salts bottle, a pair of spectacles, etc., or a "sewing" chatelaine with scissors, pincushions, needle-holders, etc., or a "religious" chatelaine with church items on the chains. The plates in silver and silverplate appeared in every variety of Victorian rococo and Art Nouveau design.

Prices depend upon size, design, and number of chains.
Silver—$35.00-$70.00
Silverplate—$20.00-$45.00

LADIES' ITEMS

AMERICAN CHATELAINE WATCHES

Silver. 10 Ligne,
Stem Wind
and Set.

Silver. 13 Ligne,
Stem Wind and Set.

Silver **$40.00-$100.00** In fine working condition

GLOVE COLOGNES

$20.00-$50.00

LADIES' ITEMS

VINAIGRETTE—SALTS BOTTLE

Silver & Cut Crystal
$20.00-$50.00
Prices Depend on Size & Design

LADIES' ITEMS

BUCKLES & PINS

In the late 1800's and early 1900's, belt buckles, girdle buckles, cloak clasps, and pins of all types were produced in an enormous variety of designs with Victorian, Rococo, and Art Nouveau dominating. Silversmiths like Unger Bros. of Newark made pin and buckle Art Nouveau designs of women's heads and figures with flowing hair and drapery.

Hair pins, hat pins, lace pins were produced in every Victorian motif and concept. Birds, animals, swords, flowers, etc. were made in Sterling Silver and often gold plated or set with semi-precious stones.

Pins
Silverplate—**$10.00-$30.00**
Sterling Silver—**$15.00-$50.00**

Buckles
$20.00-$50.00
$40.00-$100.00

Art Nouveau pieces in Silver are most valuable

All prices depend
on design,
condition &
weight of
silver
in buckles

ART NOUVEAU
circa 1900

ROCOCO-VICTORIAN
circa 1880

LADIES' ITEMS

SCABBARD PINS
Silverplate—$15.00-$40.00
Silver—$20.00-$55.00
Pins with precious stones are worth considerably more depending on type, number and quality of the stones.

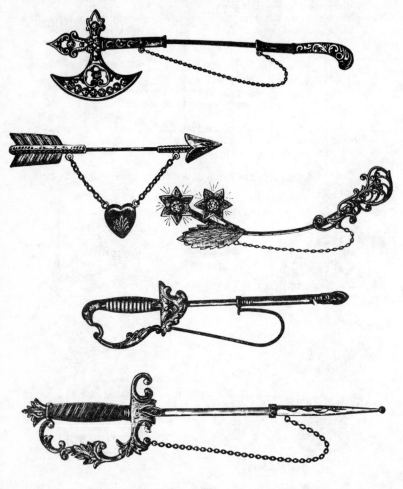

LADIES' ITEMS

HATPINS
Silverplate $10.00-$20.00
Silver $15.00-$35.00
Intricacy of design influences price

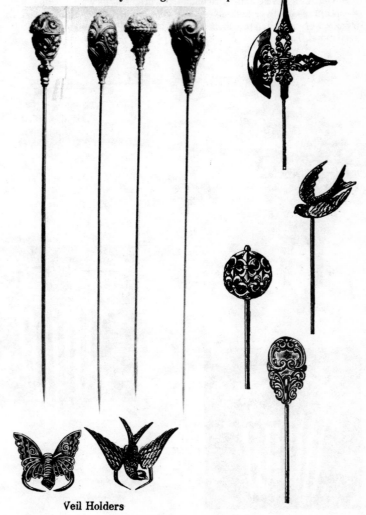

Veil Holders

LADIES' ITEMS

COMBS—PURSES

Silver decorative combs with open fretwork designs were popular in the 1880's. Mesh purses of silver and silverplate were carried for evening wear. The heavy frames were usually embellished in Victorian designs, and often the purses were suspended from chains.

circa
1890

COMBS
Silverplate
$15.00-$50.00
Sterling Silver
$30.00-$100.00

LADIES' ITEMS

PURSES
Silverplate—$35.00-$55.00
Silver—$50.00-$180.00

LAMPS

From 1850 to 1900 kerosene lamps were advertised and sold by many silver and silverplate manufacturers. The body and base of the lamp were usually decorated in Victorian designs that frequently reached a height of elaborate embellishment. The shades were often cut glass such as: Amber, Rubina Verde, Mary Gregory, etc., decorated with enameled and etched designs.

Gorham Mfg. Co. made Art Nouveau lamps in Sterling Silver embossed and chased with nymphs and flower forms.

Complete lamps with the original glass shades are very rare and valuable, due to breakage and collectibility by cut glass enthusiasts.

Oil Lamps—Silverplate
$90.00-$200.00

Depends on Size & Condition & Glass Shade.

LAVATORY SETS

Although china and porcelain were the principal materials used in making these wash table items, many Silver & Silverplate manufacturers produced Ewer and Basin sponge dishes, soap boxes, tooth brush boxes and holders in a variety of designs and styles. The Art Nouveau products of silver are the most valuable and collectable.

Silverplate—$20.00-$25.00
  Silver—$30.00-$200.00

Tooth Brush Box—$30.00-$50.00

Sponge Bowl—$15.00-$35.00

Cup—$15.00-$35.00

Soap Box—$25.00-$50.00

$200.00-$400.00

LAVATORY SETS

Martele Art Nouveau Complete Set, **$1500.00-$2500.00**
Sterling Silver, circa 1904

Silverplate Art Nouveau, Complete Set, circa 1900
$350.00-$500.00

MATCH BOXES & MATCH SAFES

MATCH BOXES

These small boxes with hinged lids were made of many materials—pewter, copper, brass, tin, nickel-silver, Sterling Silver and Silverplate, as a carrying device for inflammable phosphorous matches before the days of lighters and safety matches. They were produced in a large variety of designs and shapes from 1890 to 1910. Manufacturers such as Gorham, Unger Bros., Reed & Barton, Elgin American, Samuel Kirk, Meriden Brittania, C. W. Sedgwick, W. B. Kerr, R. Blackinton & Co., Wm. A. Rogers, etc., made many boxes in Rococo, Oriental, and Art Nouveau decorations.

Sport subjects such as fishing, hunting, golfing, baseball, football, were popular, Animal designs abounded, and often the match box itself was in the shape of an animal. Historic, patriotic, and commemorative themes were depicted and used as souvenirs of special occasions. There are match boxes with romantic paintings reproduced in elaborate embossing and chasing depicting nudes, cupids and nymphs. Unger Brothers of Newark, N.J., produced many Art Nouveau subjects; fantastic sea serpents, sea nymphs, dragons, nudes with flowing hair, noble Indians in full headdress, covered the Sterling Silver surface.

Figural boxes in the shape of a boot or shoe, a hat, a bale of cotton, a basket, an elephant's head, a horse's head, a swaddling baby, a pig, a cat, a monkey, an owl, a violin, Columbus head, a valise, etc. all are very desirable and collectable. Advertising match boxes are usually plated and carry an inscribed sales message.

Art Nouveau, Advertising, and Figural Boxes are the most sought-after at this time, and are the most valuable.

Silverplate—**$10.00-$40.00**
Sterling Silver—**$15.00-$75.00**

Price Depends on Design, Size.

Advertising Art Nouveau, Repousse, Figurals are the most valuable.

MATCH BOXES & MATCH SAFES

All Prices are for Sterling Silver
Silverplate approximately 1/2 Preces Quoted.

$25.00-$35.00 $20.00-$30.00 $25.00-$45.00 $20.00-$30.00

$15.00-$30.00 $20.00-$30.00 $40.00-$60.00   Back

$20.00-$30.00 $20.00-$30.00 $20.00-$30.00 $25.00-$45.00 $40.00-$60.00

$40.00-$70.00 $30.00-$60.00 $20.00-$30.00 $20.00-$30.00 $30.00-$50.00

MATCH SAFES &
TOOTHPICK HOLDERS

Here is an instance where the same practical product was used for a dual function, for dispensing either toothpicks or wooden matches.

A variety of human and animal motifs were the subjects of these table-top receptacles. Silver plated dogs, birds, chicks, bears, frogs and monkeys, deported themselves along with the container holding either matches or toothpicks.

Cherubs, angels, and playful kiddies held or carried the match or toothpick receptacle.

Silverplate—$20.00-$60.00

NAPKIN RINGS

A true product of the Victorian era introduced to the American public circa 1860, the napkin ring was produced by all Silver & Silverplate manufacturers including: The Meriden Britannia Company, Meriden Silver Plate Company, Reed & Barton, Pairpont Manufacturing Company, Derby Silver Company, Homan Manufacturing Company, Aurora Silver Plate Company, Acme Silver Company, Rockford Silver Plate Company, and many others.

By the 1870's hundreds of varieties and designs had appeared, the earlier simple rings in silver and silverplate decorated with engraving, engine turning, beading, piercing, and applied medallions. The origin of the figural napkin rings was as a training device for Victorian children, to encourage them to roll up their napkins and insert them in the rings. The Victorian penchant for whimsy asserted itself in these items with a veritable menagerie of animals: cats, dogs, chickens, rabbits, squirrels, goats and ponies pulling wheeled carts holding rings, turtles carrying rings on their backs, birds, butterflies, and others disporting themselves. Cherubs and playing children were also a popular motif for figural rings.

Combination caster sets with pepper shaker, salt dish and napkin ring, usually with a cherub or some other figure are valuable.

All types of figural napkin rings are very popular with collectors and dealers.

Possibly as a result of their popularity, reproductions of figural napkins are imported and sold in the U.S.

Silverplate
$7.50-$80.00
Silver
$25.00-$100.00

NAPKIN RINGS—FIGURALS*

FIGURALS
Silverplate
$50.00-$200.00

circa 1870

Silverplate
FIGURAL
$150.00

NAPKIN
RING
SET
$180.00

*figurals are the most valuable of rings

NUT BOWLS

The nut bowl is an example of art (and artisans) imitating nature. These vessels were often made in the shape of an acorn, walnut, coconut, etc., embellished with oak leaves, dragon flies, acorns, etc., and often featuring a "bright-eyed and bushy-tailed" squirrel on the rim or base. They were made by Wm. Rogers Mfg. Co., Wilcox Silver Plate Co., Derby Silver, Simpson, Hall, Miller & Co., etc. Circa 1880's - 1900's.

Silverplate $30.00-$150.00
Silver—$50.00-$200.00
Prices dependent
upon design, size,
glass insert and
weight of silver

NUT BOWL
Silverplate
circa 1880

SEA SHELL
NUT BOWL
circa 1888

NUT BOWLS

**FILIGREE
NUT BOWL
circa 1890**

See Previous Page For Prices

**SQUIRREL
NUT BOWL
circa 1890**

**VENETIAN NUT BOWL
circa 1887**

PITCHERS

Water pitchers were a popular item of Silver & Silverplate production from 1860 - 1910. The common water pitcher had no covers, unlike the double and triple wall Ice-Water Pitchers. They were also made in sets with a tray and two or three matching cups.

Elaborate designs covered the surface and handle, chased, engraved, engine turned, and embossed. The Art Nouveau period resulted in a proliferation of sinuous designs of nudes, mermaids, fish, waves, flowers, exotic animals, etc., often with matching trays.

Sterling Silver and Martelé pitchers are very desirable and valuable.

Silverplate — $85.00-$250.00
Silver — $300.00-$600.00*

Most valuable are Art Nouveau designs

"CROCUS" PATTERN
WATER PITCHER
circa 1904

*Selected pieces approach **$1000.00.**

PITCHERS

See previous page for prices

FERN DESIGN
circa 1900

**MARTELE
PITCHER
ART
NOUVEAU**

**WATER SET—SILVER
PITCHER, GOBLET, TRAY**

Fern design water pitcher. Meriden Britannia Co. catalog, no date.
Marked "Discontinued Jan. 1907."

PITCHERS

SYRUP PITCHERS

Syrup pitchers were functional table items for dispensing maple syrup or other liquid toppings, produced from the 1860's-1910. The early ones were sold with a small drip plate, eliminated in later models, containing a built-in cut-off. They were made in a large variety of designs sometimes matching a tea or coffee set.

Silverplate **$25.00-$100.00**

Syrup Pitcher & Drip Plate
circa 1870

ICE WATER PITCHERS

Before the invention and proliferation of the mechanical refrigerator, the multi-wall insulated ice pitcher was a popular table device for serving cold water. The double and treble inner walls kept the ice from melting. The outer bodies were usually made of silverplate and were embossed, chased and engraved in designs and ornaments characteristic of the Victorian period. The ice pitcher had its heyday from 1860-1900.

Because of the weight of the pitcher (ten pounds and over) tilting devices were an improvement evolved in the 1870's. The stands, goblets (One or two), waste bowls, and handles were elaborately decorated in the same motif employed on the ice pitcher.

Original complete tilting water sets are quite valuable and difficult to find.

Silverplate
$25.00-$125.00

Silver
$200.00-$500.00

Price Depends
On Size, Design
Condition, Weight of
Silver

ICE WATER
PITCHER
circa 1868

ICE WATER PITCHERS
TILTING SETS

Silverplate
$125.00 – $300.00 *
†Silver
$300.00 – $1200.00

*Price Depends
On Design, Condition,
& Weight Of Silver

ICE WATER PITCHERS
TILTING SETS

See Previous Page For Prices

PORRINGERS

These table items were made in great quantities in the 1600's and 1700's in both England and the American Colonies. The porringer was a circular shallow bowl with a decorative handle usually pierced.

Silver & Silverplate porringers were made in the 1800's but not in great quantities. Martelé Sterling Silver porringers made by Gorham in Art Nouveau designs are the most valuable of the 1800's.

Silverplate—$25.00-$100.00
Silver $85.00-$300.00

Art Nouveau Porringer

PRIZE CUPS & AWARDS

In America of the 1700's & 1800's, loving cups, prize cups, and awards were an important feature of ceremonies, presentations, and prize giving. Among the most beautiful and valuable single items of silver ever produced were mementoes of gratitude presented to victors in Americas' battles by cities, states, and private citizens. The most popular shapes for these awards were urns, vases, and bowl form centerpieces. The most elaborate molding, engraving, chasing, and repousse figures and themes covered the surface. Most of the important pieces are in museums and institutions.

Prize cups and awards (circa 1860-1910) for popular use were produced by all American silver and silverplate manufacturers. Subject matter such as sports, scholastic awards, business achievements, etc., were the basis for designs. The elaborate presentation vases, and urns in the Art Nouveau style and rising rapidly in value.

circa 1880

Silverplate $65.00-$95.00
Silver $150.00-$350.00

Silverplate $85.00-$150.00
Silver
$200.00-$500.00

PRIZE CUPS & AWARDS

Martele
Sterling Silver
26″ High—circa 1902
$1750-$3000.00

Martele
Sterling Silver
24″ High—CIRCA 1900
$2500.00-$4000.00

PUNCH BOWLS AND LADLES

The ceremonial punch bowl and set was an important part of festivities in Georgian England. From the 1860's through the 1890's it was also made by all silver and silverplate producers. The set consisted of punch bowl, tray, cups and ladle. The designs on silverplate usually centered around the grape and leaf motif.

American Sterling silver punch bowls were generally made on assignment for a commemorative occasion or the launching of a warship. So called "American Navy Presentation Silver," was donated to the warship by the citizens of the city or state after which the warship was named.

The Martelé silver pieces were one-of-a-kind examples of the silversmith's art made only by the Gorham Company. They featured Art Nouveau motifs, embossed and chased. Sea serpents, mermaids sporting in the waves, King Neptune and sea nymphs, floral and leaf motifs, satyr and nymphs covered the surface of bowl, ladle, cups and bases. Of the punch bowl pieces made in the period 1860's-1910 by American manufacturers, the Martelé examples are the most valuable.

PUNCH BOWL, CUPS AND LADLE
circa 1895
$600.00-$750.00 (Silverplate)

PUNCH BOWLS & LADLES

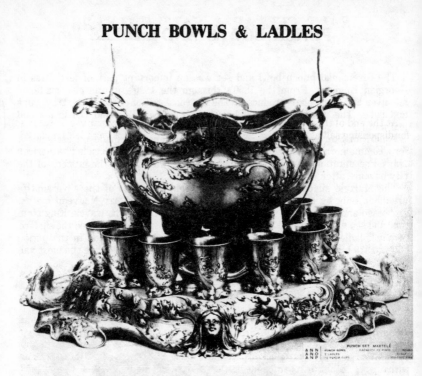

MARTELE PUNCH SET, BOWL, LADLES, CUPS, TRAY

Sterling Silver—$7500.00-$10,000.00

PUNCH LADLES
Silverplate $25.00-$75.00
Silver $100.00-$200.00

SALT CELLAR & SALT SHAKERS

At the end of the 1600's small "trencher salts" came into popular use as vessels for dispensing salt at the individual plate or "trencher." These small salts replaced the "great salt" that was the centerpiece of Middle Ages dining tables.

The early salts of the American variety were usually round, about three inches in diameter, and set on low pedestals or legs. They were decorated in the Victorian fashion with gadrooned edges, beading, chasing, and surface engraving and engine turning. The popular "lion mask" often appeared in miniature over each foot. Gilt linings or ruby glass inserts were the rule in these items. During the 1870's salts were made in diverse shapes, small round bowls and tubs with cast animal figures and other motifs. The fluted shell shape was a popular theme, and Silverplate frames in a large variety of designs with handles, and sometimes spoons, graced the tables of the period.

These open slat dishes had inserts of clear, frosted, ruby or colored glass which were often pressed or engraved.

The "Shaker Salt" (or Salt-Shaker) came into general use in the late 1870's aided by inventions and devices that prevented the salt from caking and the "Shakers" from corroding. The Victorian penchant for whimsy in small practical items asserted itself. Meriden, Brittania, Rogers Bros., Reed & Barton, Wilcox Silver, and others blossomed forth with a menagerie of cats, owls, dogs (in and out of barrels), parrots, chickens, rabbits, little Miss with Muff, little Mister with top hat, miniature champagne bottles ("Extra Dry Pepper"), and conventional shapes galore. These items were often advertised as "Peppers" since open salts were still made and used, although later catalogues defined them as "Peppers and Salts."

The "Pepper & Salt" castor sets were set on a low footed heavily decorated Silverplate frame with a center carrying handle to "pass the salt" at table. The shakers were of cut, pressed, engraved, or enamelled glass embellished with typical Victorian designs, flowers, scenery, birds, and Rococo elaborate curlicues. The pierced shaker tops were either Sterling or Silverplate.

As a group these Salt and Salt & Pepper Shakers are very collectable and desired by dealers and the public.

SALT CELLAR & SALT SHAKER
Silverplate—$6.00-$30.00 Each
Sterling Silver—$25.00-$100.00 Each

SALTS & SPOONS

SALT CELLAR

SCISSORS

All silver manufacturing companies made small sewing scissors and scissors for other purposes, such as grape scissors, poultry scissors, desk scissors, etc.

German and English steel mills usually provided the blades. The Sterling Silver handles were usually decorated in the Rococo Victorian style of scrolls and floral motifs. Unusual handles were also made, such as; grape scissors with grape and leaf design handles, stork shaped sewing scissors with the blades forming the beak, and other figural handles such as dog and hunter, double dolphin, witch of Salem, etc.

Scissors collecting is a good area for collecting interesting and potentially valuable Victorian silver artifacts.

Silverplate
$12.50-$25.00
Sterling Silver
$22.50-$60.00

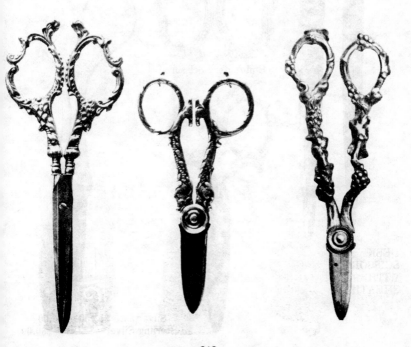

SCISSORS

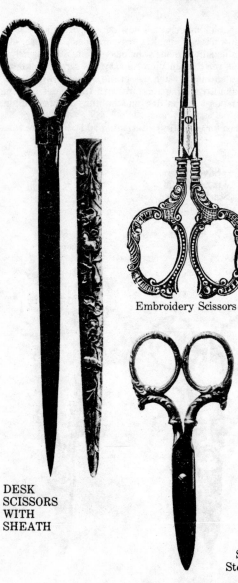

Embroidery Scissors

DESK
SCISSORS
WITH
SHEATH

Silverplate $12.50—$25.00
Sterling Silver—$22.50—$60.00

SEWING ITEMS

During the Victorian era, needlework was the chief occupation of most women. From childhood onward women were trained in all the sewing skills needed to produce table items, clothing, and decorative needlework of all types.

Silver and Silverplate manufacturers produced a great variety of items to fill this very practical and important need. Among the many products made were: Sewing sets, pin cushions, pin cabinets, spool boxes, needlecases, thimbles, bodkins and ribbon pulls, and scissors of all types.

PIN CUSHIONS

Victorian design manifested itself in the great variety of motifs used in these receptacles for needles and pins. Some were made with legs, a miniature Victorian chair for example some sat on embossed bases. Pin cushions are a desirable group of collectables and are still to be found in many antique shops and flea markets.

Prices range from $10.00-$20.00

SEWING ITEMS

SEWING BIRDS

The ladies of the 1850's to 1880's had these useful and decorative clamps to assist them in doing needlework. Made in the shape of a bird, they were fixed to the edge of a table. The beak could be opened to hold any fabric or material to be sewn. The bird carried a pin cushion on his back and one on the clamp.

Silverplate $25.00-$40.00
Sterling Silver $30.00-$50.00

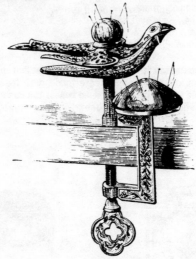

THIMBLES

Hand made silver thimbles were imported into Colonial America from Europe but by the middle 1700's American silversmiths were making them. By the mid-1800's mechanical production of thimbles was the common procedure. The borders and bands were engraved and embossed with floral motifs, or scenes of ships, houses and country views, windmills, bicycling men.

Many thimbles were made with souvenir subjects such as historic buildings and locations or World's Fair themes. Silver thimbles are readily available in antique shops, etc., and are an easy-to-collect category of Victorian and Art Nouveau.

$6.00—$15.00

SPOONS

As a group of silver and silverplate collectables, spoons offer the greatest assortment of styles, types, designs, and forms. The Victorian and Art Nouveau periods (1840-1910) saw the creation of a large variety of spoons for every conceivable table use. Aside from the table setting spoons, they were made as Berry spoons, ice cream spoons, jelly spoons, bonbon spoons, olive spoons, salad spoons, Apostle shells, sugar sifter, pea spoons, coffee spoons, Vienna coffee spoons, Apostle spoons, souvenir spoons, etc. Books have been written on the subject of spoons, and individual categories of spoons such as: AMERICAN SPOONS, SOUVENIR AND HISTORICAL by Dorothy T. Rainwater. For anyone interested in spoons these types of books are highly recommended.

The handles of spoons of all types were the object of much design and decoration. Hundreds of designs were created by the largest silverware producers, many being made in both sterling and plate. They ran the style gamut; rococo, baroque, romanesque, Victorian themes, flowers of every type, human figures such as the "Nuremberg" coffee spoons decorated with peasants and noblemen in costumes of Old Nuremberg.

Every silver production technique was used in the manufacture of spoons; embossing, casting, repousse, chasing, engraving, etching, etc. Coffee spoons, Apostle spoons, and souvenir spoons reached the height of intricate designs and figures. Beautiful enameling, gilding, and inlay work were also used extensively on coffee and souvenir spoons.

The bowls of table setting spoons were usually plain and oval in shape. Berry and salad spoons, bonbon spoons, olive spoons, sugar sifters, etc. all had elaborate piercing and cutout patterns, and scalloped and irregular edges. Stems of these spoons and coffee and souvenir spoons were often twisted and embellished.

Comic character spoons of the 1930's and 1940's with engraved or embossed figures of: Mickey Mouse, Howdy Doody, Charlie McCarthy, etc., are a popular category of silver spoons growing in value.

Complete sets of spoons, 6, 8, 12, 14, 24, etc. are much more valuable than individual items or mixed patterns.

Coin silver spoons made from melted down silver coins were extensively made in pre-1860 America by individual silversmiths. Coin silver spoons are light in weight, bowls are "egg shape," handles are usually "fiddle shape" with the owners' name or initials engraved thereon. Makers' hallmarks are stamped on the underside of the handles. Complete sets are rising in value.

SPOONS

COIN SILVER SPOONS — ROGERS BROS. 1825-61

$20.00-$30.00 Each
Set of 6
$100.00-$200.00

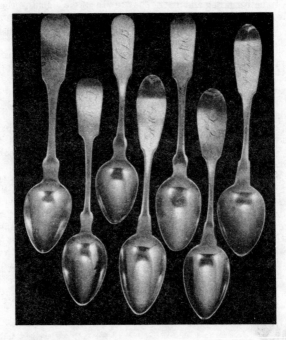

SPOONS

Berry or Salad
Silver **$15.00-$30.00**

La Vigne Pattern
Rogers Bros. 1881
Silver **$10.00-$20.00**

Salad
Silver
$30.00-$55.00

Sugar
Shell
Silver **$15.00-$25.00**

Coffee or
Souvenir
Silver **$10.00-$25.00**

Bon-Bon and Jelly
Silver **$15.00-$30.00**

SPOON HOLDERS—SPOON RACKS

Unlike the Spoon Warmer, the Spoon Holder is exclusively an American development. The two handled "Vase" shaped holder, circa 1860, stood on low pedestals and resembled miniature "Loving Cups" with restrained ornamentation. By the 1870's, Victorian ostentation in design appeared on the spoon holders.

Elaborate embossing, engraving, repousse and chasing, and classic medallions and lions heads were common as motifs.

Double spoon holders were made by most American Silverplate producers of the 1870's and 1880's. Elaborate embellished stands with castor type bail handles, some with bells or vases, held the two compartments into which the spoons were inserted.

In the mid 1870's the combination sugar bowl and spoon rack evolved. The racks on the rim of the bowl held six or twelve spoons, the sugar bowls stood on a pedestal with the cover usually crowned in a decorative finial—a bird, animal, or butterfly figural.

Spoon holders were often decorated in a matching pattern to the tea and coffee sets of the 1880's.

$20.00-$40.00*

$15.00-$50.00

*$35.00-$75.00

Prices Do Not Include Spoons

TANKARDS, MUGS, CUPS, & GOBLETS

CHILDREN'S CUPS (See page 137)

Children's cups were embellished with subjects such as: Nursery Rhymes, Clowns, Birds, Flowers, Animals, etc. They were produced in hundreds of varieties by American silver manufacturers.

GOBLETS

Goblets were widely used during the 1600's. In effect, they were flat or curved bottomed cups set on a single foot with a round base. Goblets and cups in the 1860's-1900 were made in a large variety of styles and were engraved, chased, embossed and decorated with medallions, swags, floral motifs, engine turning, etc. Art Nouveau pieces in silver have risen rapidly in price in the past years.

Silverplate $15.00-$50.00
Silver $90.00-$250.00

MUGS & CANNS

The Mug was derived from the Tankard, being slightly smaller without a cover and mainly used for drinking beer. Canns were similar to mugs differing only in being slightly larger. Form and design followed Tankards very closely. Canns are more common to the time prior to the Civil War.

CANNS   Silverplate $55.00-$145.00
          Silver $200.00-$500.00

MUGS   Silverplate $20.00-$75.00
        Silver $50.00-$100.00

TANKARDS, MUGS, CUPS, & GOBLETS

TANKARDS

Tankards of Sterling Silver were an important drinking vessel of the 1600's and 1700's usually made with a plain cylindrical body and a flat projecting rim. The hinged cover had a decorated thumb-grip to enable the cover to be opened and closed. Tankards usually had an "S" shaped handle. They were made throughout the 1800's, to early 1900's and followed the traditional form and designs.

Silver & Silverplate $100.00-$600.00

OTHER CUPS

Shaving cups, or mugs, are described and priced under "Gentlemens' Items." (page 106.) Mustache cups made of Silver & Silverplate were equipped with a guard inside the cup that kept the 1880's gentleman's mustache from dipping into the coffee or tea.

The cups and matching saucers were often elaborately engraved and these sets are the most valuable.

Mustache Cup & Saucers
Silverplate $25.00-$60.00
Silver $40.00-$90.00

MUSTACHE CUP & SAUCER
CIRCA 1895

Silver $30.00-$80.00   Silver $35.00-$100.00

TEAPOTS, TEAKETTLES, & SETS

The ceremony of tea drinking in England and on the Continent was of such importance to the nobles and the wealthy that the finest silversmiths produced beautiful examples of teapots, teakettles, and tea sets throughout the ages. If any one item can be said to represent the height of the silversmith's art, it is the teapot and teakettle and its companion pieces the sugar and creamer.

Designs of teapots and sets ranged through all periods and influences: Medieval, Renaissance, Classic, Baroque, Rococo, Queen Anne, Georgian (George I, II, III, IV) are all represented. Shapes were as varied as the designs; round, oval, octagonal, oblong, bullet-shaped, pear-shaped, inverted pear-shape, baluster shape, pumpkin-shaped, etc.

Every type of surface, decoration, casting, molding, engraving, chasing, repoussé, gadrooning, beading was employed. Tea kettles were generally globular in shape with an attached swing handle, usually on matching stand. They followed the style and design of teapots. Footed stands containing a warming lamp are found with both teakettles and teapots.

Tea pot handles were usually "S" or "C" shaped wood or silver handles attached to the body.

American teapots, teakettles and sets were made by all silver companies during the Victorian and Art Nouveau periods 1840-1910. The main design influence on Victorian items was elaborate rococo and featured repousse over-all naturalistic decorative patterns of elaborate floral detail, often combined with engraved or chased scenes of sweetness and sentiment. Curved shapes were the most popular for bodies, handles, legs and spouts. Combinations of styles were used on many Victorian pieces of silver and silverplate during the decades of 1870-1900. Designs mixing elements of Renaissance and Elizabethan, Oriental and Rococo Classic and Japanese, are often found on the same teapot and tea sets; this mixed style is also known as "Eclectic."

The Victorian and Art Nouveau Sterling Silver and Silverplate pieces are increasing in value rapidly. Complete sets with teapot, teakettle, creamer, sugar, and waste bowl are most sought after.

TEAPOTS, TEAKETTLES & SETS

Silverplate
$80.00-$300.00
Silver
$200.00-$1000.00

VICTORIAN TEAPOT
circa 1877

VICTORIAN
TEA POT
circa 1872

TEAPOTS, TEAKETTLES & SETS

TEAPOT
circa 1867

TEA KETTLE
circa 1888

TEA KETTLE
circa 1878

Tea Sets, Coffee Sets
Silverplate $75.00-$1000.00
Silver $400.00-$5000.00

TEA & COFFEE SETS

Silverplate $500.00-$1200.00   Silver $2500.00-$4000.00   circa 1867

Silverplate
$100.00-$300.00
Silver
$300.00-$800.00

TEA & COFFEE SETS

circa
1905

MARTELE
Silver
$4500.00-$7500.00

Silver
$800.00-$1500.00

TEA SETS

Silverplate
$500.00-$1000.00
Silver
$3500.00-$6000.00

Silverplate
$400.00-$700.00
Silver
$1200.00-$3000.00

TOBACCO ITEMS*

SMOKING SETS, ASH TRAYS, CIGAR AND TOBACCO BOXES

The use of tobacco and its by products, cigarettes, cigars, pipes, etc. were the basis of many collectable and interesting Silver & Silverplate items manufactured during the period 1860-1910. They were produced in a large variety of types and designs: Victorian, Rococco, Art Nouveau, etc., embossed, chased or engraved. Cigar boxes were hinged or covered, oblong or square shaped, with cast figures (often pipes) or handles on top.

SMOKER'S SETS

Consisted of cigar or cigarette receptacle, match holder, and ash tray on a matching tray, complete sets are difficult to find. They were made in both silver & silverplate in a large variety of Victorian & Art Nouveau designs.

ASH TRAYS

Often the practical feature of a cigar or match holder was combined with the ash tray. Borders were heavily embellished and cast metal cigars or pipes were frequently used as rests. Engraved humorous themes and mottos were common.

Art Nouveau ash trays in Sterling Silver, made by Unger Bros. Silversmiths of Newark, N.J., featured sensuous nudes, and ladies with flowing hair, cherubs, full face Indian Chief in headdress, smoking man, etc. These are quite rare and valuable.

CIGAR & CIGARETTE CASES

After 1900 the use of "ready-made" cigarettes proliferated. Cases to carry both cigarettes and cigars were made by many Silver & Silverplate manufacturers. Single row and double row cases were produced for cigarettes in a large variety of Art Nouveau and Rococco designs, and in the 1920's and 30's in Art Deco motifs. Cigar cases were made in the same styles and designs although they are considerably larger. Sterling Silver, Unger Bros. cases decorated in Art Nouveau motifs are most valuable and desirable.

*See "Matchboxes & Safes," pg. 192.

228

TOBACCO ITEMS
ASH TRAYS

Silver
$60.00-$150.00
Each

Silverplate
$30.00-$75.00

CIGAR &
CIGARETTE
BOXES

CIGAR LAMP
Silver
$25.00-$65.00

Silver
$60.00-$200.00 Each
Silverplate
$40.00-$150.00

SMOKING
SET

Silverplate—$25.00-$80.00   Silver—$40.00-$150.00

VANITY ITEMS

Among the most desirable, valuable, and collectable items of Silver and Silverplate are the dresser appointments and vanity items made for the ladies boudoirs of Victorian and pre-World War I America. Although individual pieces, especially mirrors, brushes, and sets are known from earlier times it wasn't until the late 1880's that matched sets appeared in many manufacturers' catalogs.

The Art Nouveau style of 1890—1910 in dresser and vanity sets were plentiful, the sets consisted of hand mirror, hair-brush, combs, whisk broom, and sometimes were made with matching nail file, tooth brush, manicure scissors, cuticle knife, shoe button hook, shoe horn and curling iron. Complete sets are hard to find, and are the most valuable of this category of collectibles.

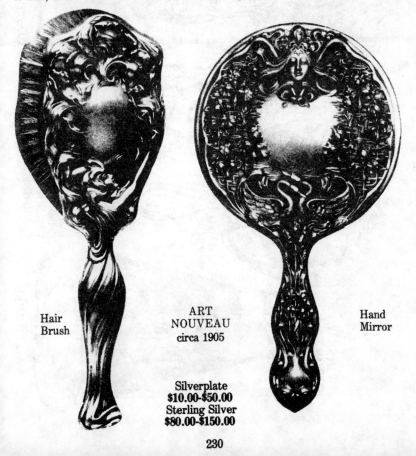

Hair
Brush

ART
NOUVEAU
circa 1905

Hand
Mirror

Silverplate
$10.00-$50.00
Sterling Silver
$80.00-$150.00

VANITY ITEMS—DRESSER SETS

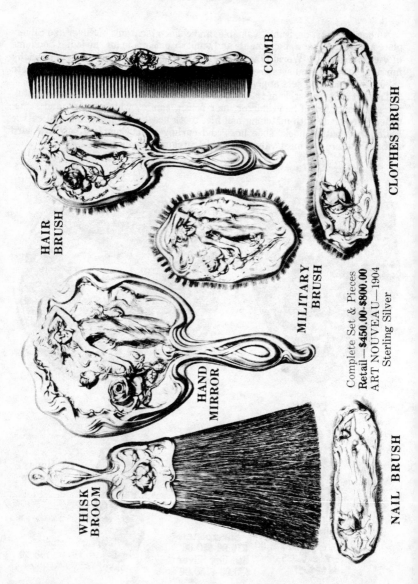

COMB

CLOTHES BRUSH

HAIR BRUSH

MILITARY BRUSH

HAND MIRROR

Complete Set & Pieces
Retail—$450.00-$800.00
ART NOUVEAU—1904
Sterling Silver

WHISK BROOM

NAIL BRUSH

231

VANITY ITEMS—DRESSER SETS
Sets Silverplate $75.00-$175.00
Silver $150.00-$350.00

Silverplate
$10.00-$50.00
Silver
$70.00-$100.00

Silverplate
$10.00-$20.00
Silver
$20.00-$40.00

Silverplate
$10.00-$50.00
Silver
$30.00-$60.00

Mustache Brush
Silverplate $10.00-$25.00
Silver $25.00-$35.00

Military Brush
Silverplate $10.00-$25.00
Silver $25.00-$40.00

VANITY ITEMS—DRESSER SETS

COMPLETE 6 TO 10
PIECE SETS IN THE
SAME PATTERN

Silver
$150.00-$350.00
Silverplate
$75.00-$175.00
Sets Are Rare

BONNET BRUSH

WHISK BROOM

All pieces on
this page
Sterling Silver
$25.00-$65.00
Silverplate
$10.00-$50.00

VELVET BRUSH

VANITY ITEMS—MANICURE SETS

Manicure sets were made in a great variety of designs around the early 1900's. Cuticle scissors and knives, nail files, polishers, corn knives, cream boxes, etc. often on a matching tray or in a fitted box. Art Nouveau motifs of flowing hair ladies and nudes, cherubs and flowers, sinuous items and leaves and asymmetrical curves were ideally suited to personal vanity items, and many handles and bodies were cast and chased in these forms.

Complete sets are difficult to find, but individual items are available at antique shops, auctions, flea markets, etc.

Individual Pieces in Sterling Silver made by Gorham Mfg. Co., and by Unger Brothers of Newark, N.J., are true and valued examples of the height of the Art Nouveau Silversmiths craft.

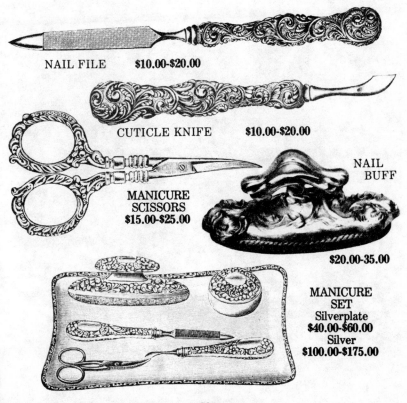

NAIL FILE $10.00-$20.00

CUTICLE KNIFE $10.00-$20.00

MANICURE
SCISSORS
$15.00-$25.00

NAIL
BUFF

$20.00-35.00

MANICURE
SET
Silverplate
$40.00-$60.00
Silver
$100.00-$175.00

VANITY ITEMS—MIRRORS

Plate-glass table mirrors made in the Victorian period are a unique and charming vanity item. Elaborately decorated with birds, flowers, angels, etc., they were made with and without covers as dressing table features, and for the wall with candle sconces. These also are scarce and valuable.

Silverplate **$175.00-$200.00**
Sterling Silver **$100.00-$300.00**

VANITY ITEMS—TOILET STANDS

Important features of the Victorian ladies boudoir dressing table were these combinations of cologne and perfume bottles, and powder puff boxes in decorative cut glass of all types in pink, blue, yellow, green, opaque and translucent colors.

Butterflies, birds, flowers, children playing (in "Mary Gregory" style) where used as decorative themes on the glass.

The stands, made of Silverplate and often gold decorated, were as elaborate as Victorian manufacturers could make them, with Egyptian, Rococo, and Classic figures and embellishments. The stands usually held three bottles, but were also known with one or two bottles and rarely, three bottles and a bud vase.

Although made in great numbers and variety during the period of 1800—1900, toilet stands are quite scarce today due to the breakage of the bottles, and their desireability to art glass collectors.

Silverplate
$30.00-$125.00
Silver
$100.00-$275.00
*Depending on Size,
Design, No. of Bottles

Worth more if
Art Glass Bottles
are present

"Mary
Gregory"
Type
Toilet
Stand

236

VANITY ITEMS—TOILET STANDS

Silverplate Single Bottle Type $30.00-$75.00

VANITY ITEMS—TOILET SETS

$85.00-$135.00

$150.00-$200.00

$60.00-$85.00

VASES & EWERS

VASES

The Victorian love of flowers and the art of bouquet-making found their proper outlets in the myriad varieties of vases produced by the Silver and Silverplate Manufacturers of America. By the 1870's elaborate ornate vases and bud vases decorated in every imaginable style were advertised and sold. Classic figurines and others proliferated: Apollo, Gladiator, Egyptian Queens and Pharoahs, Indian Chief and Squaw, Chinese Mandarin, Victorian Lady with Flower Basket, animals and birds such as deer, dogs, foxes, lions, peacocks, pheasants, canaries, cats, etc. all were either decorated on the vase, or cast as figurals on the frames and bases.

Beautiful cut glass vases on silver and silverplated mounts have been sought by glass collectors, and are quite rare and expensive. The glass vases were engraved, pressed, cut, enamelled, and decorated in every sentimental style and fashion of the Victorian era.

Peachblow, Amberina, Rubina Verde, Mary Gregory, Agata, Burmese, Amethyst, Ruby, etc. were among the types of highly desirable cut glass employed in Vases and Bud Vases.

Pottery was also used, though less frequently, in silver & silverplate mounts. The Gorham Silver Company combined elaborate pierced frames and silver overlay with Rookwood pottery vases. Rookwood pottery was art pottery made at Cincinnati by Mrs. Mabel Bellamy Storer, and other artists, circa 1880.

The pieces were often signed by the artist and always marked with the "RP" symbol and flames. Gorham also made the individual Martele vases in sterling silver with Art Nouveau floral embossed shapes and motifs.

The Rookwood and silver overlay vases, and the Martele pieces are very valuable among the finest examples of the silversmiths art.

VASES & EWERS

VASES

Silverplate $100.00-$300.00
Silver $280.00-$750.00
Prices Depend On
Type of Glass
Vase Insert

VASES & EWERS

VASES

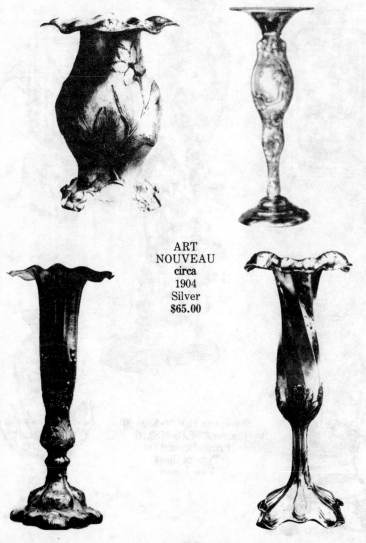

ART
NOUVEAU
circa
1904
Silver
$65.00

VASES & EWERS

VASES

Rookwood
Vase &
Silver
Overlay
circa 1901
$300.00-$500.00

Rookwood
Vase &
Silver
Overlay
$400.00-$600.00

VASES & EWERS

EWERS

These were large wide mouthed water pitchers with handles originally made in the middle ages through the 1700's. Along with the matching bowl, they were used by nobles of the times to wash their hands in a ceremonial manner. The water, often rose scented, was poured over the hands into the basin.

The helmet shape of the ewer with a curved spout and an "S" shaped handle often in the form of a sinuous female figure was made during the Art Nouveau period. The Gorham Sterling Martelé Ewers and plateau are fine examples of these items, with embossed, repousse and chased figures and wave forms, Rockwood pottery vases encased in Art Nouveau Sterling fretwork, were also made by Gorham, and are quite scarce and valuable.

EWERS   Silverplate $75.00-$250.00
        Silver $200.00-$750.00

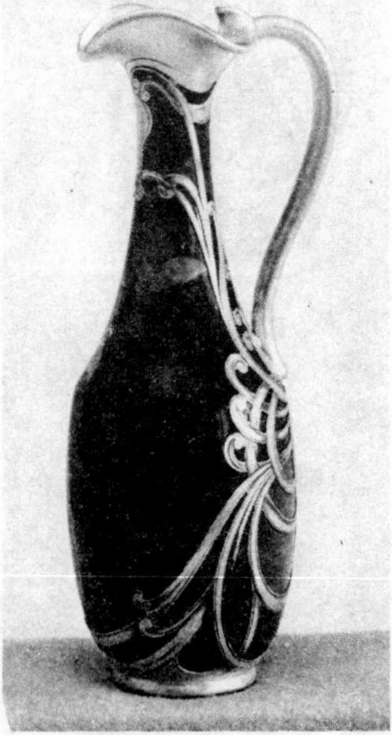

ART
NOUVEAU

circa 1901

Rookwood
Ewer
& Silver
Overlay

12" High

$300.00-$500.00
Each

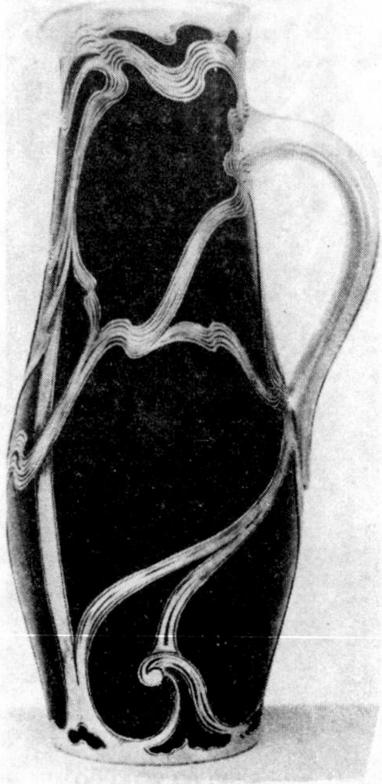

WAITERS, TRAYS AND
SALVERS

The waiter and salver were trays used to serve tea, coffee, punch, etc. Shapes in Silver and Silverplate were generally oval, but also were made round, square, rectangular. During the Art Nouveau period shapes were eratic and irregular. Waiters shaped to curve around the body when carried were used in the 1870's. The borders were the focus of design and embellishments with beading, gadrooning, egg and tongue, rococco motifs, piercing, engraving, chasing, and repousse work. Center surface ornamentation, when used, was chasing or engraving with the designs often matching those on other items used in serving. Special purpose trays include bread trays, sandwich trays, crumb trays, children's trays, pin and trinket trays, etc.

Art Nouveau trays by Unger Brothers, and Martelé trays made by Gorham in Sterling Silver embellished with naturalistic floral motifs, flowing hair ladies, exotic fish and mermaids, are very desirable and valuable.

VICTORIAN
circa
1870

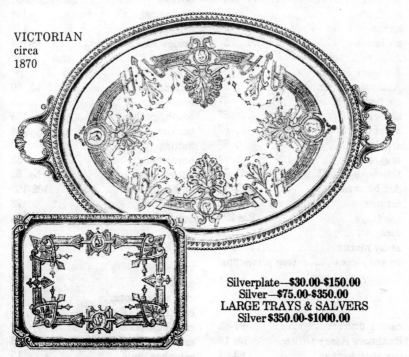

Silverplate—$30.00-$150.00
Silver—$75.00-$350.00
LARGE TRAYS & SALVERS
Silver $350.00-$1000.00

Price Depends on Size, Design & Weight of Silver.

A